MAKING YOUR LAWN & GARDEN GROW

a Melnor guide to indoor and outdoor gardening

by Elvin McDonald

Dorison House Publishers, Inc., New York

Copyright © 1977 by Dorison House Publishers, Inc.

Published by Dorison House Publishers, Inc.

183 Madison Avenue, New York, N.Y. 10016

ISBN: 0-916752-07-0

Library of Congress Catalog Card Number: 76-48843

Manufactured in the United States of America

TABLE OF CONTENTS

Chapter 1

ESSENTIALS FOR HEALTHY PLANTS

There are hundreds of thousands of different kinds of plants, each of which, at least theoretically, has a precise set of needs to promote optimum growth. In practice, most plants are tremendously adaptable provided they have certain essentials.

And what are the essentials plants need in order to survive? Light, nutrients, water and reasonable temperatures are the basics, each of which will be discussed in this chapter. Understanding these is easy, largely a matter of common sense. What gets confusing is deciding the specifics—in other words, the best kind of light for the plant you want to grow, the soil that will nourish healthy growth, the proper amount of water and a temperature range that will not kill, either from heat or cold.

Beyond these basics, it helps if plants have protection from pests and diseases. In terms of the global balance of nature, this is a human invention that is not absolutely essential. However, you will be a much more successful gardener if you know how to doctor your plants, either preventively or when the need arises, and for this reason the basics of plant pest and disease control are also included in this chapter.

If you are interested primarily in indoor gardening, read this chapter first as an overview to the basics of light, nutrients, water, temperatures and protection from pests and diseases, then turn to Chapter 8: Bringing in the Outdoors for more specific information about house plants.

Basic Plant Need #1: Light. All plants need light in order to grow, but some need less than others. The range outdoors is from full, direct sun all day to areas that receive little or no direct sun because they are shaded by trees or buildings. However simplistic it may sound, the most important thing to learn is the difference between direct sun and shade. If this puzzles you, think of yourself: You lie in full sun to get a sun tan, but if you want to feel cooler on a hot summer day, you seek the shade of a tree or the shadows cast by a building or tall fence.

In the various chapters of this book, the specific light needs of all kinds of plants—from towering trees to creeping ground covers—are given. You'll also find suggestions about the light needs of plants in other books, seed and nursery catalogs and increasingly on the labels local garden centers use to tag everything from flats of annual flowers, vegetables and herbs, to big nursery stock.

In the strictest sense, **full sun** means direct sun all day long, for example, in the middle of an open field, but in a yard or garden, virtually all plants that need full sun will do well in a half day or more. In other words, a piece of ground facing southeast, south or southwest qualifies as being in full sun if no tall trees or buildings block off the direct rays of light. Most trees need a half day or more of direct sun as do flowering shrubs such as lilacs, forsythia, viburnum and roses. Vegetables, herbs and fruit-bearing plants such as apple trees, raspberries and strawberries also need a full half day or more of sun. Lawn grasses such as bluegrass and Bermudagrass need full sun, as do such annual and perennial flowers as zinnia, marigold, peony and Shasta daisy.

Full shade, like full sun, is relatively easy to define. If less than an hour of direct sun reaches a place where you want to grow plants, consider that it is in full shade. Not as many varieties will grow in this kind of light as in part to full sun, but within every major category of plants, excepting vegetables and fruits, there are kinds that will thrive in shade. Specific examples and recommendations are given in the various chapters of this book.

Between full sun and full shade lies the sometimes confusing kind of light we refer to as **part sun** or **part shade**. Any area that receives several hours of direct sun, but not a full half day, may be classed as receiving part sun. In practice, a lot of plants that ideally need full sun will adapt quite well to part sun, especially in a climate that is usually hot and mostly cloudless in the summertime.

Part shade is the term used to describe an area that receives a maximum of three hours direct sun, or a place that is shaded by tall, fairly open trees that permit patches of direct sun to reach the ground for brief periods through the day. Numerous small flowering plants do well in this kind of light, for example, impatiens, fuchsias, browallia, wax and tuber-ous-rooted begonias. Flowering shrubs such as mountain-laurel, rhododendron and azalea will also grow in part shade, or what is sometimes called dappled sunlight. Ground covers such as hardy ferns, myrtle or periwinkle (**Vinca minor**), English ivy, pachysandra, and even certain lawn grasses such as the creeping fescues will thrive in part shade. And, while most trees need full sun, flowering dogwood and redbud will do nicely in the part sun or part shade found beneath tall shade trees that form a leafy but not dense canopy of foliage overhead.

Most gardens offer a variety of light conditions, from full sun to full shade. As you work outdoors around your property, you will just naturally begin to know how much sun or shade reaches different parts of the garden at various times of the day. Once you have these in mind, you can take advantage of what in effect are little climates that are uniquely suited to certain kinds of plants. In other words, if you put the right plant in the right kind of light, your chances for success with it will improve considerably.

Basic Plant Need #2: Nutrients. The roots of most plants commonly grow in soil which not only provides them an anchor but gives nourishment in the form of nitrogen, phosphorus, potash and a diet rich in minerals and other trace elements. Soil, dirt or earth is not actually necessary for plants. They will also grow in water, sterile vermiculite, perlite, sand or even wood shavings, provided the vital nutrients are supplied to the roots. Growing plants without soil is variously referred to as soil-less or hydroponic culture, and while an increasing number of gardeners are experimenting with this technique, most gardens in the foreseeable future will be cultivated in soil.

There are some easy tests to make on the soil around your garden to see if it is promising or in need of improving. One is an ancient, proven, rule of thumb: If healthy weeds grow on a patch of ground, it will also grow ornamental or edible plants.

The second way to find out about soil is sometimes called

the trowel test: Take a garden trowel to the piece of ground where you want to plant something; insert the blade into the soil as deep as you can by using only one hand on the handle. If it slips down easily to a depth of four or five inches, you are probably fortunate enough to have soil that will grow healthy plants and be easy for you to dig in and cultivate. If it is difficult to push the blade of the trowel into the ground, the soil may be rocky or merely hard from too much clay content and not enough sand or humus.

A third way to get a feel for what kind of soil you have is the squeeze test. Take a handful of soil that is moist, but neither wet nor powdery dry. Squeeze it tightly, then release your grip. Soil of the proper consistency will break out of the ball when you touch it lightly with your index finger. If it does not break, this is a sign that the soil contains too much clay and needs to have some sand and humus (well-rotted compost or sphagnum peat moss, for example) mixed with it. If the handful of soil does not hold a ball shape at all after squeezing, it is probably too sandy and needs a boost in the form of humus.

There are of course more scientific ways to test soil. One is to buy a soil-test kit and do the research yourself. If a chemistry set was what you liked to play with as a child, you can have a lot of fun as you experiment with a soil-test kit. The easier way if you're not inclined to chemistry is to have a complete soil test made by your County Agent who is a local representative of the United States Department of Agriculture; a small charge may or may not be made for this service. Or, you can have this testing done through your State Experiment Station, another arm of the United States Department of Agriculture. The addresses for these are listed in the text which follows. If, for example, you live in Virginia, you would address your letter of inquiry about soil testing to the Virginia State Experiment Station, Blacksburg, Virginia.

Guide To State Experiment Stations

Alabama: Auburn	Nebraska: Lincoln
Alaska: College	Nevada: Reno
Arizona: Tucson	New Hampshire: Durham
Arkansas: Fayetteville	New Jersey: New Brunswick
California: Berkeley	New Mexico: University Park
Colorado: Fort Collins	New York: Ithaca
Connecticut: New Haven	North Carolina: Raleigh
Delaware: Newark	North Dakota: Fargo
Florida: Gainesville	Ohio: Columbus
Georgia: Athens	Oklahoma: Stillwater
Hawaii: Honolulu	Oregon: Corvallis
Idaho: Moscow	Pennsylvania: University Park
Illinois: Urbana	Puerto Rico: Rio Piedras
Indiana: West Lafayette	Rhode Island: Kingston
Iowa: Ames	South Carolina: Clemson
Kansas: Manhattan	South Dakota: College Station
Kentucky: Lexington	Tennessee: Knoxville
Louisiana: Baton Rouge	Texas: College Station
Maine: Orono	Utah: Logan
Maryland: College Park	Vermont: Burlington
Massachusetts: Amherst	Virginia: Blacksburg
Michigan: East Lansing	Washington: Pullman
Minnesota: St. Paul	West Virginia: Morgantown
Missouri: Columbia	Wisconsin: Madison
Montana: Bozeman	Wyoming: Laramie

In practice, most yards offer soil that will grow thriving plants without too much expense or labor on your part, especially if you are careful to provide extra water during seasons when there is not enough natural rainfall. The biggest problem usually occurs when soil is a sticky clay in a low-lying area where excess rainfall cannot run off quickly. Very few plants can grow in such a boggy patch of ground.

A somewhat lesser problem occurs when you want to grow an acid-loving plant such as a rhododendron or azalea in soil that is strongly on the alkaline side. If in doubt, the pH of the soil can be determined by the simplest of soil-test kits, but if you have a complete test made on your soil, the results will show the pH as well as the nutrients it contains—or needs. Most of the plants we grow require a pH between 5.5 and slightly above 7.0, the numbers below 7.0 representing soil on the acid side, and numbers above 7.0 representing soil on the alkaline or "sweet" side.

Basic Plant Need #3: Water. It hardly seems necessary to say that plants cannot live without water, but in fact they can no more survive without it than we can. It's true, of course, a water-lily needs a lot more than a cactus from the desert, but even a giant cactus cannot survive indefinitely without a good drink of water. For this reason, it is vital that the water needs of each plant be considered before you try to make it grow in your garden. And, you will be a much more successful gardener from the very beginning if you invest in the proper watering equipment for the size of your garden and the kinds of plants you want to grow. You will find specific recommendations for all kinds of plants in the chapters which follow.

If you live in an arid climate, but water is in plentiful supply, you can select almost any plant and irrigate it sufficiently in dry seasons to sustain healthy growth. If, on the other hand, you live in a dry climate where the water supply is limited, grow as many native or drought-resistant plants as possible. Concentrate water-loving plants in a small enough area for you to be able to irrigate them when they need it.

Growing desert plants in a wet climate is also possible,

usually by situating them in raised planting beds. This technique doesn't keep moisture from reaching the roots, but it does hurry up the run-off so that they are on the dry side much more rapidly than those of plantings made directly in the existing terrain.

Because water is a vital element in gardening, we have prepared the accompanying charts. Study them and you will be able to decide which pieces of equipment or accessories will help you grow a better garden—for less work. Without the proper watering equipment, a long period of dry weather can turn your garden dead, or at best wear you out from trying to water thirsty plants without the right kind of help.

Traveling Sprinklers

☐ **Traveling Sprinkler:** Lay out the hose in any area you want to water; the traveling sprinkler will follow wherever the hose leads, even up and down hills and around corners, watering in a circular pattern as it moves slowly along, and automatically shuts itself off.

Oscillating Lawn Sprinklers

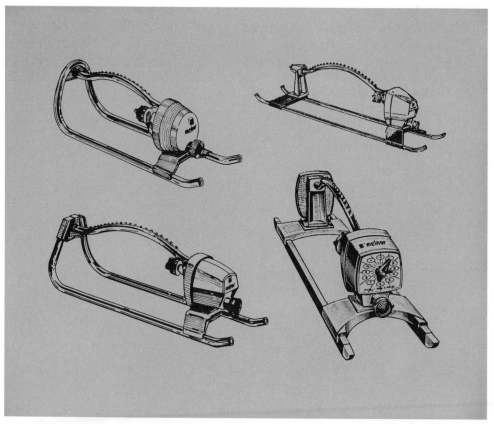

☐ **Oscillator:** Gently waters a rectangular-shape area—
or any portion of it.

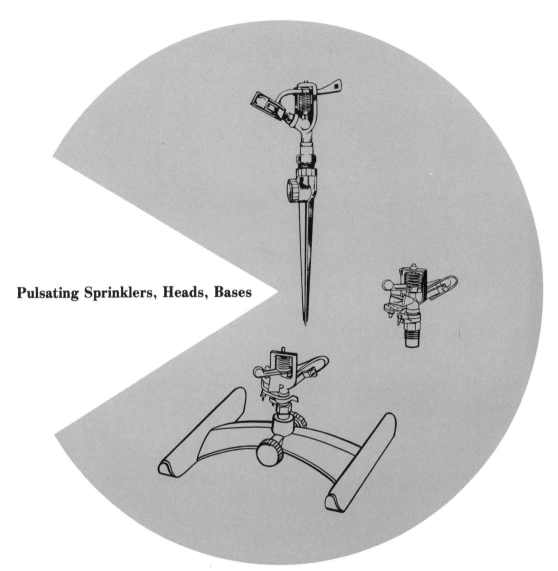

Pulsating Sprinklers, Heads, Bases

☐ **Pulsator:** Waters in a low pattern relatively unaffected by wind. Waters in a full circle or any part of it—a pie-shape wedge, for example, or half circle.

Revolving, Specialty Sprinklers

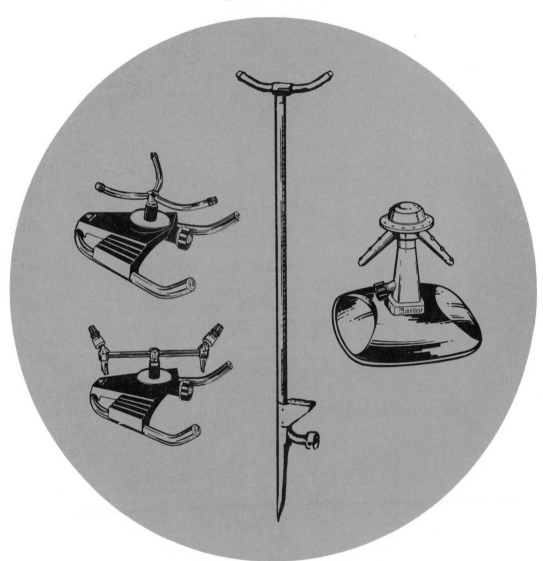

☐ **Revolving Sprinkler:** Waters in a full, circular pattern.

Turret Sprinkler/Stationary Sprinklers

☐ **Specialty Sprinklers:** Consider these for watering odd-shaped places, or small inaccessible areas, such as a long, narrow strip between a driveway and house.

Accessories

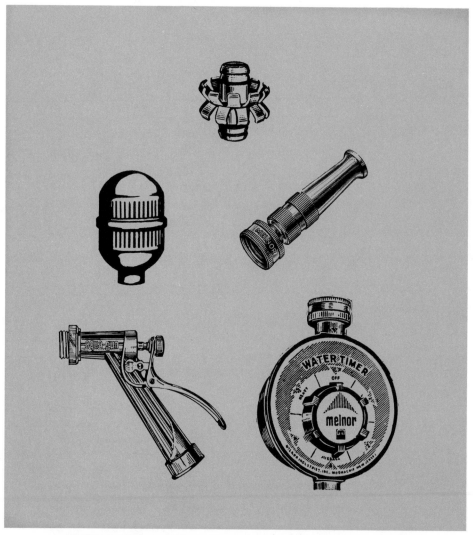

☐ **Water Timer:** You can use one of these with any sprinkler. Simply set the dial to the number of gallons of water you want applied to any given area; on completion, the water will be shut off automatically.

Basic Plant Need #4: Reasonable Temperatures. It is an overgeneralization to say that all plants can be divided into two groups, those that can survive freezing temperatures and those that cannot, but in the broadest sense this is the way it is in the green world. The complication lies in the fact that some plants can survive temperatures of 28 degrees F., but not one degree less. Others can survive temperatures 40 degrees **below** zero, yet they will not live indefinitely in a climate where freezing temperatures never occur.

One guide you can use in selecting plants that are suited to living all year outdoors in your climate is to determine the zone in which you live by studying the Plant Hardiness Zone Map (see illustration), prepared by the United States Department of Agriculture. These same zone numbers are used by many nurseries, both mail-order and local, to designate the cold hardiness of plants.

PLANT HARDINESS ZONE MAP

APPROXIMATE RANGE OF
AVERAGE ANNUAL MINIMUM
TEMPERATURES FOR EACH ZONE

ZONE 3 -40° TO -30°
ZONE 4 -30° TO -20°
ZONE 5 -20° TO -10°
ZONE 6 -10° TO 0°
ZONE 7   0° TO 10°
ZONE 8   10° TO 20°
ZONE 9   20° TO 30°
ZONE 10 30° TO 40°

17

Another guide to help you determine plant hardiness is this: If the variety in question is frequently cultivated as a house plant, it is probably not able to withstand freezing temperatures. Some examples that come readily to mind are begonias (excepting one species, **Begonia evansiana**, the hardy begonia), impatiens, jade plants, caladiums and Swedish ivies.

In order to plan your gardening activities, it will help if you know the average date for the last frost in the spring where you live, and the average date of the first killing frost in autumn. You can secure this information by writing to your State Experiment Station, the address for which is listed earlier in this chapter. These dates are especially important if you want to grow vegetables, because some of them, lettuce, radishes and onions, for example, do best when planted early in the season, even before the last frost is expected, and others won't grow until the weather is settled well above freezing.

One other rule of thumb may help you in selecting plants to grow outdoors all year in your climate: If you live where winter brings freezing temperatures, the plants you see growing outdoors in the tropics are not likely to survive where you live unless you can bring them indoors for the duration of freezing weather. Conversely, if you live in the tropics, most of the trees, shrubs, and even some perennial flowers such as peonies, you see in the North are not likely to transplant well to your balmy clime.

Basic Plant Need #5: Protection from Pests and Diseases. In nature, survival of the fittest is the rule, but when we invest money, work and even love in growing a plant, most of us don't want it to be eaten alive by bugs, caterpillars or bandit raccoons any more than we want it to die from a disease. One encouraging fact to keep in mind is that the healthier a plant is from receiving proper light, nutrients, water and temperatures, the less likely it is to fall prey to either a pest or a disease.

Today there are basically three philosophies about controlling pests and diseases among plants. One is the totally organic approach in which no potentially harmful pesticides are used. At the other extreme is the increasingly less popular solution of using both chemical and natural pesticides to knock off or cure the malady of the moment.

The third approach is a middle-of-the-road attitude of sensibility: Use the right pesticide if everything else fails. Determining which pesticide is right may sound like a difficult thing to do, but it needn't be if you read the fine print on the bottles and boxes of plant-care products at your nursery or garden center. Environmentalists universally discourage the use of one-shot-does-it-all multi-purpose sprays. The logic behind this recommendation makes sense. Why coat your plant with a combination insecticide, miticide and fungicide when in fact it may need only one, not all three?

Some Beneficial Garden Insects

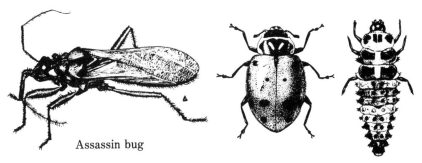

Assassin bug

Adult and larva of lady beetle

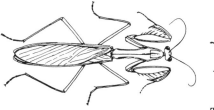

Praying mantis

Tiny wasp depositing egg in an aphid

Insect Pests

Earwig

Lawn Chinch Bugs

Clay-Backed Cutworm

Fall Armyworm

Leafhopper

Bagworm

Birch Leaf Miner

Rose Aphid

Mealy Bug

Blister Mite

Spider Mite

Slug

Spittle Bug

Flower Thrip

Cucumber Beetle Enlarged

Colorado Potato Beetle Enlarged

Tent Caterpiller

Black Cutworm

Imported Cabbage Worm

If you can't decide whether your plant in distress needs an insecticide, a miticide, a fungicide, or merely a strong fence to keep out hungry animals, discuss the problem with a neighbor who gardens, or with someone at your local nursery or garden center. If these sources don't give you the answer, get in touch with your County Agent (usually listed in the Yellow Pages under United States Government offices) or your State Experiment Station, the address for which is listed earlier in this chapter.

Chapter 2

PLAN YOUR LANDSCAPE
TO ESCAPE WORK

Gardening is a combination of little and big satisfactions, surprises, even triumphs you simply can't comprehend until you get in there and start digging. And some of the best digging you can do is on paper—thoughtful planning to make your outdoor spaces really work for you. Mistakes made on paper are a lot easier to correct than when they are made with actual plants or structural materials. Study this chapter, then tailor your own landscape design, one uniquely suited to the lifestyle of you and your family.

Development of exterior landscape spaces is not unlike building and decorating a house. Graded land represents the foundation. Surfacing materials become the floor. Trees, or vines trained on an arbor, are the roof. Shrubs, fencing, or structural screening become the enclosing walls. Your goal is to organize these elements well so that the landscape functions for you. Every site is unique, but the fundamentals of good design are constant.

First, measure your property. Two can do this a lot easier than one person working alone. You'll need a long measuring tape, some sheets of graph paper on a clipboard, and a pencil for making on-the-spot notations.

Determine scale—for instance, ¼ inch equals 1 foot—and indicate on your worksheet all major structures and plants. When complete, your plot plan will show the exact placement of the house, walks, driveway, trees, outbuildings, plus any noticeable slopes in the lay of the land. Especially if you anticipate changing the grade, or a major excavation for a swimming pool, you should indicate on your plot plan the placement of sanitation and water lines, along with overhead or underground electrical wires.

Once you have your plot plan neatly and accurately sketched, you can begin to consider the three basic areas found in home landscapes: (1) public garden or access area; (2) living or private area; and (3) service area. This breaks your design task into three projects, and while you want all to interrelate and work together in the final plan, it is easier to begin by working out the details for each specific area.

It will help your planning if you study other landscapes

living or
private area   service area   public garden
or access area

around you. For example, will symmetrical or asymmetrical balance do more for the entry of your home—and you? It is possible to use either approach successfully; perfect symmetry simply conveys a feeling of more formality (see sketches).

What to do with cars—yours and those of visitors—is a major concern in landscape planning. Approached from a design ideal, you will have a turn court (the hammer-head shape is most common) which allows you to enter the street head on, and parking that allows cars to leave without having to move others. Plan so that the car is directed away from the house entrances and walks when backing, to avoid pedestrians and children at play.

If your property is not large enough to allow a turn court and off-street parking, keep in mind these suggestions: Keep plant materials low so they do not interfere with vision when you back into the street. Make the drive wide enough to allow a turning radius that doesn't require backing across traffic lanes. Avoid having a drive that is steeply graded. It will always be a liability, hazardous for parking, impossible in bad weather.

Place your walkway to the main entrance for maximum convenience from the parking area. Avoid having a center walk and driveway running parallel to the street with no connecting walk, otherwise you will have a hard-packed, grass-less strip worn between. Much better is to have an entry garden with a spacious, all-weather surface for sure-footed access from the parking space to the front door.

There is an old saying that goes this way, "Architects don't make mistakes, they plant trees or vines," and it holds a world of truth. Or from an optimistic viewpoint, you can landscape with purpose.

For instance, let's say you've just moved to a new development where a utility pole and lines give a harsh view both inside and out. Trees are probably the answer. Maybe an evergreen to block out the lower part of the pole, and some leafy flowering or shade trees between the house and the street to help you forget the wires.

Or maybe you have a fireplug that seems to sit in the middle of your picture window. It has to be clearly on view from the street, but not from inside your house. So you plant a screen of shrubbery between your window and the fireplug.

If your property has a relatively narrow side-yard, try to make it a functional part of your working landscape. How about a deep gravel or stone mulch overall with stepping stones for a walkway? This eliminates lawn maintenance in an area where grass probably isn't needed anyway. If you can make it easily accessible to the street, this is a good place for trash-can storage and clothesline, perhaps a storage cabinet for yard and garden tools. Or, you can put in a deep mulch of rubber tire or bark chips overall and install a jungle gym, sandbox and slide for your youngsters.

Trees and other plantings can do wonders for the most ordinary kind of house. For example, a split level. Trees can frame the building and create a feeling of balance. Shrubs and other low plantings mask the foundation, and extend outward on either side, unifying all the elements into a pleasing whole (see sketches).

A low, one-story ranch house looks better with shade

trees smaller than might be planted around a split level or a two-story colonial. Smaller trees placed to the side and in back of a low house on a small property help to create an illusion of spaciousness (see sketches), especially if there are taller trees toward the back of the lot.

If your property is already landscaped, either recently or by a previous owner, be sure you know what you want and need before ripping things out, doing more planting, or attempting outdoor construction. The landscape you inherit is likely to be a high-maintenance trap. If so, first decide what plants you want to keep, then proceed, but slowly, making the changes that seem necessary. If possible, save any particularly beautiful plantings but be most concerned with the overall long-range appearance and the use of your property. Once you've put your plan on paper, put it into action. Transplanted city people often attach a sentimental value to every tree and bush they have. If your plantings are not useful or attractive or require heavy maintenance, they really must be rearranged or disposed of. Whether it is the driveway or a rosebush that isn't in the right place, move it or get rid of it.

Maintenance Traps To Look For

1. Scattered plantings of shrubs or perennials, around the house, or here and there on the lawn.

2. Attractive plantings wasted in places not readily visible from outdoor living areas or from windows inside.

3. Large areas of lawn where grass isn't really needed for practical or esthetic reasons.

4. Grass on any steep area difficult to mow.

5. Small, broken-up lawn areas with sharp angles, which require extra backup work with the mower.

6. Large, rampant shrubs near the house that require frequent prunings.

7. Plants under a wide overhang where constant watering is needed since rain doesn't reach there.

8. Trees of a kind subject to attacks by insects or diseases, or "dirty" trees that constantly drop leaves, bark,

seeds or fruit.

9. Plants that are struggling or require extra attention to survive because they are tender for your region or just naturally difficult.

Essentials for a Low-Upkeep Landscape

LAWNS. Restrict grass to areas of play, for the formal entrance, or as a foreground for a flower border. Use edging strips to keep grass in a neat line out of flowerbeds and to avoid hand trimming. Plant ground covers in heavy shade or excessively wet soil. Remove grass from around the base of trees; replace with wood or brush chips. Get rid of small, chopped-up areas of grass and sharp angles difficult to mow. Use ground cover on steep slopes. Install an automatic underground sprinkler system or invest in a quality Melnor oscillating, pulsating or Travel-Matic® traveling sprinkler.

FLOWERS. Depend on flowering shrubs, spring bulbs and hardy perennials. Mass together. But not too many. Enough for impact outdoors. Mulch to avoid hand weeding. Use containers of annual-flowering plants for movable color— where you want it at the moment. Don't fuss with a big flower garden otherwise. For cutting to make bouquets indoors, grow in rows in a sunny, out-of-the-way corner where everything doesn't have to be kept in perfect order.

ENTRIES AND SIDE YARDS. Design with clean lines for a well-groomed look with little care. Select broadleaf and needle evergreens. In a side yard, or where there is a wide overhanging eave, mulch with pebbles, gravel or woodchips. Result? Neat appearance, no upkeep.

DRIVEWAY AND PARKING AREA. Asphalt or concrete requires less maintenance than gravel. Gravel tends to work away and to require replacement; however, process gravel with an over-coating of pea stone can be serviceable. Bricks may also be used for an attractive surface. Place the parking area so it isn't on view from the house or from the outdoor living room. Outline the area with a bumper strip so that cars will not be driven onto grass. Light the drive and parking areas at night. If the driveway is long or difficult to navigate at night, install reflectors to assist.

PATIO, TERRACE, SUNDECK. Extend your house out into the landscape as far as possible by the use of permanent-surfaced outdoor living areas. Use wood, brick, stone, pebble-surfaced concrete, or tile to make the house seem larger and cut down on outside maintenance. Consider sun, shade and the prevailing winds. Plan to eat in different spots. A terrace for breakfast or brunch should catch the morning sun. A terrace for noontime or early evening meals needs protection from southern and western sun. Terraces used in early spring and late fall need protection from chilling winds. Consider one large terrace for evening entertaining of a few friends, or a crowd—probably more people than you would ever have inside. Buy weatherproof furniture that doesn't have to be painted and won't rot. Avoid anything with cushions you have to take in at night or when it rains. If inexpensive aluminum and plastic furniture best fits your budget, select all in one color that blends into the landscape.

SWIMMING POOLS. Place a pool away from any trees that constantly drop leaves or seed pods, try to fit it naturally into the landscape, preferably so that your winter view from the house won't be directly into a frozen or canvas-covered pool. Design wide areas of permanent surfacing around the pool for sunning and eating. Pools require maintenance but this space might otherwise be in grass, which is no picnic either.

CHILDREN'S PLAY AREA. Should be on view from where you work in the house so that young children may be supervised from inside. Provide an open lawn space for rugged games but no grass under the swing set or around the sand pile. Instead, set down shredded bark or reclaimed rubber tire bits to save work—and skinned knees. Plant shrubs without thorns, or screen with a solid fence such as redwood or stockade.

OUTDOOR COOKING. Locate conveniently near the kitchen. Buy a small portable unit. Most places don't have space for a built-in barbecue pit with a chimney. More desirable today, a neat hibachi. All too often the outdoor cooking equipment becomes a focal point in the landscape. Be sure it isn't ugly. A small unit is easily cleaned and can be moved from one area to another to enable you to eat in different places depending on the occasion and the time of year. Avoid placing the unit over lawn grass because spilled lighter fluid discolors or may kill spots of grass.

TOOL STORAGE, GARDEN WORK CENTER, UTILITY. Proper tools help keep garden work at a minimum. What you need is the right tool in good shape, stored where it belongs. Try to incorporate tool storage and a work center into a unit that also performs some landscape function—maybe to screen an unsightly view, garbage pails, a drying yard or compost heap. Locate conveniently for moving the lawn mower, snow plow and wheelbarrow. Design with permanent surfacing. Screen from public view and outdoor living area. This utility area can also incorporate a drying yard, a dog pen and a place to store fireplace wood. Garbage cans recessed in the ground if possible. Plan a faucet in the area and night lighting.

Putting Your Landscape Plan on Paper

Depending on the size of your property, and the sheet of graph paper, decide on what scale to use. This might be 1/4 inch to equal 1 foot, or 1 inch to equal 10 or 20 feet on a larger property. Various graph papers are divided differently; you may be able to simply let one box equal 1 square foot.

Indicate on the graph paper the exact locations of any existing buildings, driveways, walks, fences, walls, paths, major trees and shrubs, power lines, poles, easements and rights-of-way. It is not necessary to draw in every tree and shrub, but rather you may indicate them as masses where they are grouped. It is useful to show the trunk placement of a large tree as well as the approximate branch spread. Indicate the direction North, so that patterns of sun and shade can be determined.

When this plan is complete, slip it under a sheet of tracing paper (from an art supply store). Now you can sketch out ideas by the hour without messing up your master plan. When a completed new plan takes shape on a tissue overlay, transfer it to a new sheet of graph paper. When you consider it finished, have several photostatic copies made. You will need one for working with in the garden, one for inside, and one to take to the nursery when you buy. It won't hurt to have some extras.

By the time you reach the point of putting that first sheet of tissue over your master plan, you will have an accumulation of landscaping ideas in your head and also roughed out on notepaper. Doodling in miniature is an excellent way to try out a lot of ideas without feeling self-conscious as you may on a large sheet of tracing paper. Do final sketching to scale of any miniature that is appealing.

As you plan, keep foremost in mind the low-upkeep concept. Within this framework, you want outdoor spaces that are livable and attractive. Strive for strong, clear design that will be pleasant to look at and live in. Professional landscape designers often define spaces by the use of wide mowing strips, raised planting beds and low walls. These built-in features maintain the basic design even after years of plant growth. Think in terms of plant masses rather than specimens. Later, when the overall design is complete, you can decide where to put each plant of your choice.

Most landscaping designs combine curves with right angles. Serpentine curves, crescents and circles pleasantly lead the eye, and in a long narrow lot they can do all kinds of tricks to create illusions of space. Grass areas defined in curves make mowing easier.

It is also possible to design partially or entirely within a modular concept, using only rectangles or squares. By this approach, you will take one basic unit, say 4 x 4 feet, and repeat it over and over. The patio could measure four 4-foot modules one way, seven the other, for a 16 x 28-foot total. One or more of the modules might be used as a planting pocket, the others paved. Walks and planting beds will be 4 feet wide, or in multiples of the basic 4 x 4 unit. If the modular approach appeals to you, try it. There may well be no quicker or easier way for you to achieve an attractive landscape design.

For areas involving shrubs and trees or the construction of walls, fences or buildings, it will be helpful to make elevation sketches. These show a two-dimensional view. For example, by working with the builder's elevation plans of your house, or large photos of it, you can make tissue overlays to try out various plant groupings in relation to a particular door or set of windows.

After you finish your complete design on paper, it may still be difficult for you to imagine how it will look in reality. Next best is to build a scale model. This is time-consuming but enjoyable work, especially in winter, and a far better way to discover faults in the plan than after it has been executed on the site in concrete, cash and sweat. For the model you can use cardboard, clay, blocks of wood, bits of ceramic tile, evergreen clippings and twigs.

The major consideration when designing your landscape plan is to enhance your home and make outdoor living more pleasurable. Modern architecture, with its many sharp corners, is not a pleasing thing to the eye. When landscaping, select shrubs that will soften the corners or any sharp entries of the house. Try to maintain in your planting as many curved lines as possible so that no formality develops. Use shrubs that will grow in a manner that does not require constant shearing or other maintenance. Also keep in mind the color of your house and any surrounding structures as you select plant and flower colors.

Chapter 3
LAWNS AND OTHER GROUND COVERS

If you want the best lawn on the block—forget the low-upkeep concept. A perfectly manicured lawn requires a yard slave—either you hire one or become one. However, you can have a decent lawn with minimum maintenance requirements if you choose the right grass, prepare the soil properly, and keep the lawn basically healthy.

Choosing the right grass is important to success in building a new lawn because each species has certain requirements of temperature, light, water, nutrients and other growth essentials that make it more suitable for one area than another.

Lawn grasses are grouped into cool-season and warm-season types. Cool-season grasses make their maximum growth during the cool months of the year. Although they remain green in the summer, they are semidormant then and exhibit only limited growth during this time. Warm-season grasses are those that make their maximum growth in warm months. Most of these grasses do not survive winter in northern areas. With few exceptions, they turn brown with the first frost and remain dormant or at least semidormant until spring.

The accompanying map shows the sections of the country where cool- and warm-season grasses grow best.

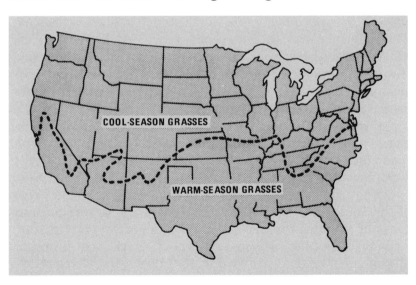

Your local nursery or garden center will probably carry only grasses that are adapted to your region. Let's take a look at the most desirable cool- and warm-season grasses, with an eye to their maintenance needs.

Most cool-season grasses sold today come in a mixture. This may be confusing to you, but the mixtures have been prepared with purpose. Conditions vary from one area of your lawn to another, and in each area, the species that succeeds best will take over; in addition, some of the grasses in each mixture are more susceptible to certain diseases than others, and when a susceptible species succumbs to a disease, one of the more resistant strains will take over.

When you are buying grass seed, it is definitely not the time to economize. As a matter of fact, beware of cut-rate seeds. For example, high-quality Merion Kentucky bluegrass is quite expensive, but there are inexpensive Merion mixtures on the market. However, these will occasionally contain as little as 1 percent actual Merion. This doesn't mean that you should buy according to price or even name brand. Check the label for the mixture inside. The label on a box of lawn seed is most important. By law it contains the actual amount of all seed contained in the package.

Avoid mixtures containing large amounts of annual ryegrass. It sprouts quickly, but, as the name implies, it does not generally survive into the second year. Should some plants last in favored locations, they become coarse and clumpy. However, a **small** percentage of ryegrass is useful when covering a newly seeded slope, since it will give quick cover for protection while perennial grasses get established.

Forget mixtures with even a small amount of coarse grass, unless you are sowing them in an old field that is already full of weeds. If you want an attractive lawn, you really must sow only fine-textured grasses.

Kentucky bluegrass is the basic grass for northern areas of the country. It is a hardy, long-lived, thick turf-forming grass of medium texture. Prominent selected varieties are Fylking, Ken-blue, Merion, Newport, Park and Windsor. Merion and Windsor are two of the most popular varieties.

Both have good tolerance to close mowing and hot weather. However, they require a high level of fertility, and Merion is subject to leaf rust and mold in shaded areas.

Red fescue, next to Kentucky blue, is the most popular cool-season lawn grass. It is excellent for shade and will survive with little water and fertilizer. Familiar varieties include Chewings, Highlight, Pennlawn, Ranier and Ruby. Fescue is slow-growing, but it will resist considerable wear.

A mixture of 70 percent creeping red fescue and 30 percent bluegrass makes an excellent minimum-maintenance lawn of cool-season grasses.

Bentgrass, of all the cool-season types, makes the most beautiful turf. It forms a dense uniform mat of rich green. But if you yearn for low upkeep, forget it, unless you restrict your lawn to a very small area where you can have that putting-green look. Bentgrass requires frequent mowing, ample feeding, pest control and occasional thinning. Some suggested varieties include Penncross, Seaside, Astoria, Exeter, Colonial and Kingstown.

The textures and looks of warm-area grasses vary greatly, so they are rarely sold in mixtures. It is therefore even more important in Southern regions to choose carefully when selecting the grass for your lawn.

Bermuda is the number one grass of the South. It grows vigorously and forms a low dense turf that tolerates heat and close mowing. Bermuda may be popular, but it demands regular attention: monthly feeding and twice weekly mowing at low height. Common Bermuda grass cannot endure shade and is the only strain established by seed. The others like U-3 and Tiflawn are propagated vegetatively.

Zoysia, once established, is among the finest Southern lawn grasses. It makes a thick cushiony sod that resists most afflictions. It can stand moderate shade, close clipping and does not require much maintenance. Zoysia is very slow to grow, and even when established does not have to be cut often. Most popular varieties are Meyer and Emerald. They are propagated vegetatively. Zoysia requires less attention than Bermuda.

Centipede is not the most elegant of grasses but it will result in what can be termed an "adequate" Southern lawn. It actually resents too much attention, and prefers acid soils. Centipede can be established from seed, but most often is vegetatively propagated. It grows well in shade and on poor, sandy soils.

St. Augustine is a coarse-textured but not unattractive grass popular in coastal areas from the Carolinas to east Texas. It is tolerant of shade and adapted to mucky soils and warm, moist climates. Sod can be purchased inexpensively. Unfortunately, St. Augustine is susceptible to disease, to invasion by chinch bug and other difficult-to-control maladies. The problems are compounded because it is not tolerant to 2,4-D and arsenate weedkillers.

Bahia is popular in the deep South because it is relatively carefree, tolerant and can be started from seed. It thrives in most soils in shade or sun with moderate attention. For low maintenance, Bahia is better than St. Augustine, and for looks it tops centipede. The Argentine variety produces fewer difficult-to-mow seedheads than the more prevalent Pensacola.

Carpetgrass requires soil with high moisture content all year long. It spreads rapidly and produces dense, compact, coarse-textured turf. It can be established by seeding, sprigging and laying sod. For Gulf Coast only.

Dichondra, widely used in southern California, is a grass substitute for warm-area lawns. It has rounded, heart-shaped leaves on trailing stems. Dichondra is beautiful, requires little mowing, but needs frequent feeding and watering. Start from seed or sprigs, but don't attempt to grow it if temperatures in your area go below freezing.

Installing a New Lawn

If you want an easy-care lawn, make it healthy at the start and then keep it that way. To borrow an adage, "As the soil is prepared, so grows the grass." Grass derives life from sun, soil, and water. You can't do much about the sun, but you can improve the soil. A properly prepared soilbed will give the lawn the right start because grass roots will spread easily. Later it will reduce the problems and costs of the mature lawn.

First determine the present condition of your soil. There are two methods. You can send soil samples from different parts of the lawn area to your local county agent or state agricultural extension service (check the Yellow Pages). Or you can buy an inexpensive soil testing kit and do it yourself. With either method, the soil samples will tell you the conditioners needed to add to the soil, the acidity level and how to raise and lower it, and the kind and amount of fertilizer to be added.

Rent a rototiller to loosen the soil so that it can be worked. Don't work soil when it is wet. When tilling, avoid beating the soil into a fluff. Fluffed soil forms a compact mass when wet. Remove stones larger than 2 inches in diameter and debris. The soil must be graded evenly so there are no pockets in which water can collect. The slope should drop gently away from the house for proper drainage. Use a hand rake for leveling and spreading.

Now is the time to make use of the information from your soil testing. Additives may include lime, superphosphate, peat moss, well-rotted manure, fully decomposed sawdust, sewage sludge, peanut hulls or rice hulls. Do a thorough job of incorporating additives into the soil. Failure to do so will create layers that may cause future trouble. Then add a complete fertilizer (one containing nitrogen, phosphorus and potash). Rake it lightly into the soil. Add 25 pounds of a complete fertilizer with a ratio of 20-10-10 or 12-8-6 for each 1,000 square feet of lawn. The numbers on the fertilizer bag identify the percentage of each component in the mixture. All brands use the same order, first nitrogen, then phosphorus and finally potash.

Once you have added the fertilizer and double-checked to make sure there are no low spots, you are ready to consider the grass.

There are three methods of establishing lawn grass:

seeding, sodding and vegetative planting. The method you use will depend on the type grass you choose and the rapidity of cover desired. Seeding is the cheapest method and does not require much work; sodding gives an instant effect but is comparatively expensive; vegetative planting requires work but is the only way to start some excellent low-maintenance grasses, such as zoysia and centipede.

The best time to sow cool-season grass seed is the fall. Early spring is best for warm-season types. Cool-season types may also be started in early spring. If you are caught without having seeded by the time early summer rolls around and you don't want to spend the hot weather with a dustbowl on your hands, sow a temporary lawn of ryegrass and then in the fall plow it under as fertilizer before planting a permanent grass mixture.

A mechanical spreader is the safest and quickest way to broadcast seed. The seed package gives the correct setting. It will also tell the coverage possible with the seed you have. Divide the seed in half and spread the first half over the entire lawn area using the spreader setting at one-half the recommended opening. Use the second half of the seed by walking crosswise. If you walked north and south the first time, then go east and west the second. Now use the back of your rake or a light roller to bring the seed in contact with the soil.

Mulching with a light covering of barn or salt-marsh hay will help hold moisture and prevent washing away the seed during watering or rain. Apply evenly and lightly. The grass will grow through the mulch, which will rot and add fertility to the soil.

New seedlings should be kept moist until well established. Once seeds have begun to germinate, they must not dry out or they will die. Light and frequent watering during a seven- to 14-day period should be sufficient. An oscillating sprinkler is excellent for this purpose.

Since we don't recommend grass for steep slopes or terraces, the expense of sodding is seldom justified unless complete coverage is needed immediately. To sod, prepare and fertilize the lawn area in the same way as for seeding. Then firm it with a light roller. Sod should not be more than an inch thick. Three-quarter-inch sod will knit to the underlying soil faster than thicker sod. Fit the squares or strips tightly together. After laying the first strip, use a broad board for kneeling to avoid tramping on the prepared seedbed.

Once the sod is laid, tamp it lightly. Then water regularly and deeply. After it is rooted, topdress with a well-mixed and screened mixture of topsoil, sand and organic matter. Fill in cracks between sod pieces with a broom or the back of a wooden rake.

Seed for warm-season grasses such as zoysia, St. Augustine, centipede, and certain improved Bermudas is not available or does not produce plants that are true to type. These grasses must be planted vegetatively by plugging, strip sodding or sprigging.

Plugging means planting small plugs or blocks of sod at measured intervals, generally 12 inches apart. They may be set closer together for more rapid coverage. The plugs should be planted tightly in prepared holes and tamped firmly into place.

Strip sodding involves planting strips of sod, 2 to 4 inches wide, end to end in rows 12 inches apart. Firm contact with surrounding soil is necessary.

Sprigging is the planting of individual plants, runners, cuttings or stolons at spaced intervals. Sprigs or runners are obtained by tearing apart or shredding solid pieces of established sod. The space interval is governed by the spread-rate of the grass, how fast coverage is desired and the amount of planting material you bought. Lawns may be sprigged at any time during the growing season when adequate moisture is available.

Lawn Maintenance with Low Upkeep in Mind

When the snow melts, remove the winter's accumulation of dead grass, leaves and other debris that can choke off sunlight and water.

Apply a complete fertilizer—one containing nitrogen, phosphorus and potash—in early spring and fall. Read the instructions carefully and apply evenly so you don't "burn" the grass. Follow with an extra application of nitrogen in late spring for cool-season grasses. Warm-season grasses will require feedings of nitrogen every four to six weeks through summer. Most lawns, particularly those east of the Mississippi River, should have applications of lime every two or three years.

Apply a pre-emergent crabgrass killer in March or April. Apply a broadleaf weedkiller in May or June. Both the fertilizers and weedkillers are easy to apply with mechanical spreaders, but follow manufacturer's instructions for rate and time of application.

Cool-season grasses should be cut at 1 1/4 to 1 1/2 inches during the spring to thicken the turf so that it can combat crabgrass more effectively. As warm weather sets in, raise the height-of-cut to a range of 1 1/2 to 2 1/2 inches and maintain it at this level for the rest of the growing season. Cut warm-season grasses normally at heights 3/4 to 1 inch. Closer cutting during the spring will encourage lateral growth and turf density.

Water during the hot summer months. When needed, water deeply to encourage deep rooting of the grass. Frequent shallow watering draws roots to the surface, weakens the plant, and encourages weeds.

In early fall check for compaction. If it exists, rent an aerator and run it over the lawn.

Set up your maintenance program and then follow it. Healthy grass is easy-care grass.

HOW TO IDENTIFY COMMON LAWN WEEDS

Plantain

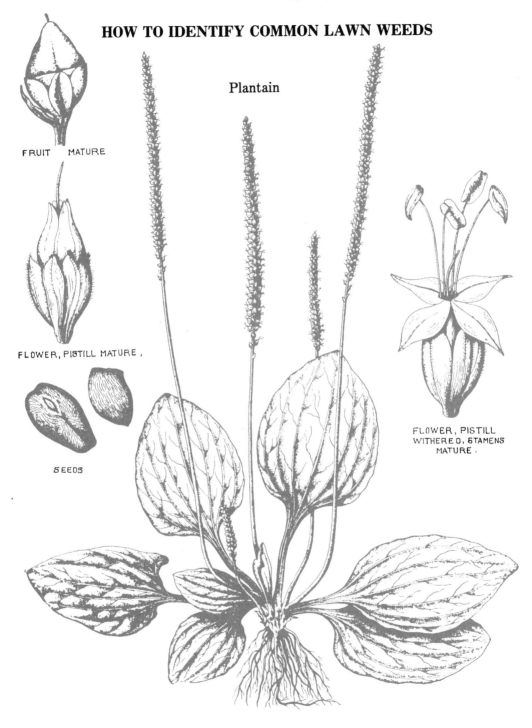

FRUIT   MATURE

FLOWER, PISTILL MATURE,

SEEDS

FLOWER, PISTILL
WITHERED, STAMENS
MATURE.

Goosegrass

Sheep Sorrel

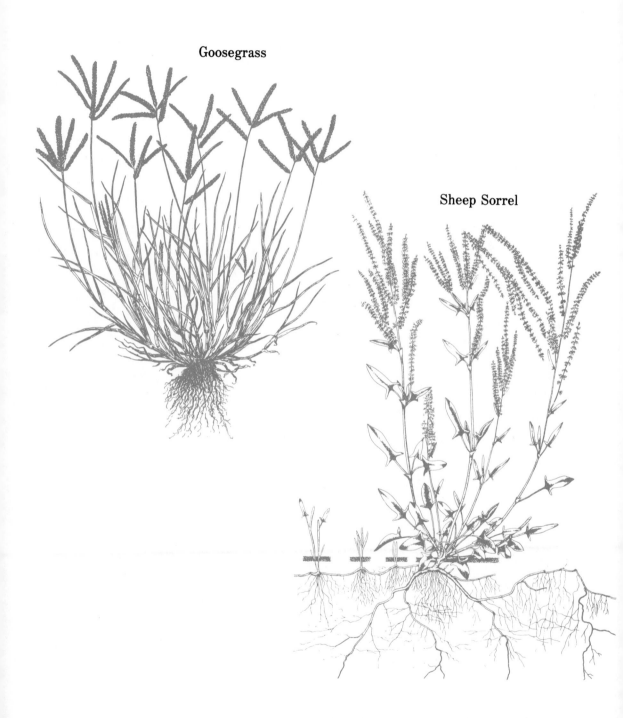

Mouse-Ear Chickweed

Nimblewill

Buckhorn

Where NOT to Have a Lawn

If grass won't grow in an area because of too much shade, if a slope is too steep or too rocky to mow, if you have too much lawn and already enough permanent surfacing, your answers may be mulches and special plants to use as low-upkeep ground coverings.

Where a mulch—such as wood chips, stones or pebbles—can be used, the least possible upkeep results. Spread it over bare spaces between trees, shrubs or in flower beds. A good mulch conserves soil moisture, stabilizes soil temperatures and keeps down weeds.

Select a mulch material on the basis of availability and appearance. Subdued earth colors are best. The light color of, say, white gravel can become a glaring distraction. The idea is that a mulch will save time, produce better plants, and be of pleasant appearance. Fresh sawdust takes so much nitrogen from the soil that you have to add about a pound of nitrogen to each 100 pounds of dry sawdust you put down. But if sawdust is plentiful in your area, and inexpensive, it may be worth your while to use it and add the fertilizer. Never put down a mulch that is likely to contain weed seeds—straw, for example, which might have bindweed or other noxious weeds. Know your source.

In recent years, the mulching trend has been to small stones, gravel or wood chips. Hardwood bark chips make an ideal organic mulch, easy to apply and maintain. They are not costly, and with a little aging turn a rich dark brown. Chips vary from $3 to $5 for 3 cubic feet, enough to cover 9 square feet 4 inches deep. Apply at any time. These chips also make natural-looking paths and walkways and are useful under children's play equipment.

To make the most effective use of a mulch, first clear the area to be covered. Remove all weeds. Then lay black or clear plastic over the area. Make cutouts around existing plants or, after laying the plastic, make holes where plants are to be inserted in the soil. Then spread the mulch. Plastic keeps weeds to an absolute minimum, yet adequate moisture seeps in around plants and through the places where strips overlap.

If the terrain is steeply sloped, wood chips will not stay in place; then planting with a bank-binding plant is your answer (see later in this chapter).

Heavy tar roofing paper is also used to keep out weeds in an area of trees and shrubs. Camouflage this unattractive material with wood chips, stones, pebbles or gravel. Edge the area with a brick mowing strip, preferably set with mortar, so that hand-trimming will not be needed and the mulch stays cleanly where it belongs, not mixing in with the grass, or spilling into the walkway.

Another helpful place for a mulch is along the drip-strip of a house that does not have guttering. Gravel, or another absorbent mulch, such as redwood bark chips, laid 6 to 10 inches deep, soaks up the runoff immediately, and permits the use of the strip area as a walkway—instead of making it a place where plants are beaten to the ground in an ugly strip of eroded soil.

Some warnings about mulch materials: Dry peat moss can be impermeable to water. Dry peat and straw can be fire hazards. Lawn-grass clippings belong nowhere except on the compost heap. To take them directly from the mower and place on a flowerbed is to invite disease and a most unpleasant odor. In windy climates, cocoa-bean and buckwheat hulls may blow away.

Ground covers are another alternative way of handling an area where grass is difficult to grow or mow, as on a steep slope or in heavy shade.

The best plants for the purpose make a solid cover. They should be of a type to propagate easily, generally growing not above 12 inches, and in most situations, sturdy enough to be walked over at least occasionally. The best ground-cover plants thrive in a wide range of soil and moisture conditions, and are relatively free of pests and disease. Three kinds that meet these requirements are myrtle (*Vinca minor*), pachysandra and English ivy. These and others are discussed at the end of this chapter.

After selecting a ground cover, prepare the soil as well as your strength, time and money allow. Good preparation eventually means less work. Work in fertilizer; 3 to 6 pounds of 5-10-5 to each 100 square feet will do nicely. Incorporate plenty of peat moss, well-rooted manure, leaf mold, sand or compost, particularly in sticky soil. Add lots of extra humus if the soil is sandy. If you can't manage this preparation over the entire area, then improve the soil for each planting hole.

Determine how close to plant. If quick cover and erosion prevention are your aim, set plants close together, for example, 12 inches for English ivy and pachysandra. For very steep or difficult areas, choose a creeper that roots at the nodes, English ivy, for example, or a woody plant with an abundance of horizontal, ground-hugging stems; Hall's honey-suckle is good but can become a pest if growing conditions are too encouraging.

Ground covers can be a natural extension of a clipped lawn area, but for a neat appearance with less upkeep, design clean divisions between the casual ground-cover habit and the clipped formality of a lawn. Consider pachysandra. Never was there a more widely planted ground cover, except English ivy. Yet pachysandra gets a bad name when it is allowed to spread into a straggly line at the lawn's edge. It needs a structural outline, a brick or metal mowing strip, so that it can't wander carelessly into the grass.

Wherever you have a large expanse of ground cover, it is possible to interplant with spring-flowering bulbs. For deep ground cover—to 10 inches tall—select the taller daffodils. In a flat, low ground cover, plant grape-hyacinths, crocus, scilla and chionodoxa. You may also interplant fall-blooming crocus, colchicum and sternbergia.

The cost of a ground cover for a large area can be prohibitive, but you can always start with a few plants, and propagate them by cuttings or division. For these starter plants, prepare the soil extra well, keep it moist, and feed lightly but frequently to get rapid growth. Of course, if your neighbor has an established stand of a choice ground cover that needs thinning, you can do him or her a favor by carefully pulling out some of the older plants for your own use.

Perennial Ground Covers

Aegopodium podagraria variegatum. Goutweed. Deciduous. Sun or shade. Spreads by creeping rootstock; 12-15 inches high. A nearly indestructible plant, or, in other words, a terrible weed except for unlimited areas.

Ajuga reptans. Bugleweed. Evergreen to semi-evergreen. Sun or shade. Spreads by stolons; 4-8 inches high. When established, discourages weeds. Forms dense mat. For quick cover, space 6 inches apart. Flowers in attractive purple, blue or white spikes in spring.

Asarum canadense. Wild ginger. Evergreen. Shade. Spreads by underground rootstock; 6-8 inches high. Attractive kidney-shaped, cupped leaves. Thrives in moist, rich, woodsy soil.

Asperula odorata. Sweet woodruff. Deciduous. Partial to full shade. Succulent, fresh green leaves give off pleasant scent of new-mown hay when crushed underfoot; 8 inches high. Excellent in rocky, wooded areas.

Bergenia cordifolia. Deciduous. Sun to partial shade. Creeping clumps form colonies of thick, heavy leaves; 12 inches high. Excellent in moist, woodsy, wild situation.

Callirhoe involucrata. Buffalo-rose or poppy-mallow. Deciduous. Sun. Trailing plants; 6-8 inches high. Lobed leaves like a true geranium. Dark-crimson flowers 2 inches across in summer. Plant divisions in spring. Extremely deep-rooted; drought tolerant.

Ceratostigma plumbaginoides. Plumbago or leadwort. Deciduous to semi-evergreen. Sun to partial shade. Creeping stems; 6 inches high. Abundant blue flowers in early fall. Foliage does not appear until late spring.

Comptonia peregrina. Sweet-fern. Deciduous shrub; 3 feet. Sun. Bank-binder. Transplant from the wild with lots of roots. Keep moist until established. Aromatic foliage.

Convallaria majalis. Lily-of-the-valley. Deciduous. Open or deep shade, but not much bloom without some sun. Well-established plants spread rapidly by underground rootstocks; leaves 6-8 inches high. White, fragrant flowers in spring. Should not be walked on.

Cornus canadensis. Bunchberry. Evergreen. Shade in moist, peaty soil. Starry white flowers in late spring. Creeps by underground rootstock; 6-8 inches high. Thrives in cold climates.

Dianthus deltoides. Maiden pink. Deciduous to semi-evergreen. Sun. Creeping, mat forming; 6-8 inches high. Flowers in early summer, and sometimes later through season. Can also be increased by seed.

Epimedium macranthum. Barrenwort. Deciduous (foliage browns in fall but persists through winter). Shade. Spreads; 9-12 inches high. Elegant and airy, best in moist, woodsy soil.

Euphorbia cyparissias. Cypress spurge. Deciduous. Sun. Spreads quickly; 8-10 inches high. Rough, dry areas; steep banks. Tends to woodiness, but useful in the right place.

Fragaria chiloensis (or hybrids). Strawberry. Deciduous to semi-evergreen. Sun. Spreads by stolons and forms a dense mat 3-6 inches high. Needs thinning every two or three years.

Lysimachia nummularia. Moneywort, Creeping Charley, Creeping Jenny. Deciduous. Sun or shade. Creeper, 2-3 inches high. Yellow flowers in summer. Tends to spread and mix into the lawn unless curbed.

Hemerocallis. Daylily. Perennial, mostly deciduous; some less cold-hardy varieties are evergreen in the South. Sun to partial shade. Grassy clumps, to 24 inches high, with flowering stems rising taller in season. Excellent bank-binder; may be used to control area where erosion is a problem, if planted 12-18 inches apart, and established at first by rocks or logs placed at intervals.

Liriope muscari. Lily-turf. Evergreen. Winter-hardy south of Washington, D.C. Sun or shade. Spreads by underground stems. Coarse, grassy clumps, 10-15 inches high. Lavender flowers in August.

Mitchella repens. Partridge-berry. Evergreen. Shade, even dense. Creeping stems take root along the ground; 4-6 inches high. White flowers, followed by bright red berries in early autumn. Propagate by seed or division. Grows slowly, but a beautiful ground cover in a wooded area.

Ophiopogon japonicus. Dwarf lily-turf. Evergreen. Sun or shade. Spreads by underground stems. Grassy leaves form a sodlike mat, 8-12 inches high. Also called *Mondo japonicus*.

Pachysandra terminalis. Japanese spurge. Evergreen. Sun or shade. Spreads; 6-8 inches high. Glossy, dark green leaves. Plant 8 inches apart for quick cover. Propagate by cuttings.

P. terminalis 'Silveredge' with white-marked leaves is interesting for a lighter shade of green to relieve a large expanse of ground cover in a shaded area. Plants in full sun need more watering and feeding than those in shade.

Phlox subulata. Moss-pink. Evergreen. Sun. Creeps, each plant forming a large dense mat; 6 inches high. Flowers white or in vivid shades of pink, red or lavender in spring. Avoid the violet magenta variety. Ideal for rocky banks where stems can cascade.

Polygonum reynowtria. Fleece-flower. Deciduous. Sun. Spreads rapidly by underground stems; 12 inches high. Sprays of lacy flowers in autumn, at first dark red, change to pink. Light green leaves turn red in autumn.

Polystichum acrostichoides. Christmas fern or evergreen fern. Shade. Fronds to 24 inches high, form mats. Evergreen to January. Fine for rocky banks and crevices.

Ranunculus repens. Creeping buttercup. Deciduous. Sun to partial shade. Spreads by runners; 6-8 inches high, with yellow flowers in spring on stems to 24 inches. Useful for moist places. Given a chance, it will spread into lawn areas.

Sedum. Stonecrop. Evergreen (semi-evergreen in cold climates). Spreads rapidly by trailing stems, too invasive to be grown near less dominant plants. To 6 inches high. Unusually fine for dry, sun-baked places, especially **Sedum acre, S. sarmentosum**, and **S. sexangulare**.

Sempervivum. Houseleek or hen and chicks. Evergreen to semi-evergreen. Sun. Spreads by offsets. Leaves form neat low rosettes. Especially useful for a sandy or rocky bank.

Thymus serpyllum. Creeping thyme. Deciduous. Creeping stems covered by tiny leaves form large dense mats; 2-4 inches high. When stepped on, gives off a pleasing fragrance. **T. s. coccineum**, with reddish purple flowers in late June, is probably the best of all thymes for covering ground in sunny, hot, dry places. Evergreen leaves turn bronze in autumn.

Veronica latifolia. Creeping veronica. Deciduous. Sun to partial shade. Spreads by creeping stems; 4-6 inches high. Pale-blue flowers in June over dark foliage. **V. rupestris** spreads into a solid mat; gives sapphire-blue flowers in May and June. Drought tolerant; competes well with weeds.

Vinca minor. Periwinkle or myrtle. Evergreen. Partial to full shade. (In sun, winter burn may be a problem.) Needs fertile, humusy, moist soil for best results.

Viola (V. odorata and various American species). Hardy violet. Deciduous. Will grow in full shade, but won't bloom as much as in partial sun. Native violets make excellent ground covers in shaded moist places. Self-sow abundantly; given opportunity, they do spread into lawn areas, otherwise they are easy to grow, and pleasant throughout the growing season. Need ample water in late summer.

Woody Ground Covers (Subshrubs)

Arctostaphylos uva-ursi. Bearberry. Evergreen. Sun to partial shade. Creeper; 4-8 inches high. Dark green leaves. Grows well by the ocean in sandy soils. Sometimes difficult to get started.

Calluna vulgaris. Heather. Evergreen. Sun. Upright, shrub to 12 inches high. Needle-like leaves. Prune out old wood in the spring. Soil on the acid side, humusy. Spikes of pink flowers in autumn.

Cotoneaster dammeri radicans. Littleleaf cotoneaster. Evergreen. Sun. Prostrate creeper; 12 inches high. Excellent on banks or other large areas. Also **C. horizontalis** (prostrate or rock cotoneaster). Semi-evergreen to deciduous.

Erica carnea. Heath. Evergreen. Sun. Spreading or upright shrubs; to 12 inches high. Very small leaves. Spikes of white or rose-pink flowers in early spring. Needs soil on the acid side, humusy and well-drained. Clip out dead wood in the spring after flowering.

Euonymus fortunei. Wintercreeper. Evergreen. Sun to partial shade. Trailer, 10 inches tall. Heavy, dark green foliage. Variety **coloratus** has vivid reddish purple leaves in autumn. **Minimus** has tiny leaves. **Reticulatus** has variegated green-and-white leaves. Use on slopes and banks. Will eventually climb walls and trees, by means of aerial rootlets.

Gaultheria procumbens. Wintergreen. Evergreen. Light shade. Creeper; 3 inches high. Small, shiny leaves. Thrives in rich, moist soil in woods.

Hedera helix. English ivy. Evergreen. Sun to shade. **Hedera helix baltica** (Baltic ivy) is hardiest, and recommended for colder climates. Plant well-rooted cuttings 12 inches apart. If stems are long enough, pin them down with wire bent to hairpin form, or hold down with small stones, so that roots along the stem will take hold. The old saying about ivy is worth remembering: The first year it sleeps, the second it creeps, and the third it grows by leaps. It burns if exposed to winter sun but recovers if cut back in spring. Moist, humusy soil is conducive to luxuriant growth.

Helianthemum nummularium. Sun-rose. Sun. 6-12 inches high. Use in a dry place.

Hypericum calycinum. St. John's-wort. Sun to partial shade. Clumps spread by underground rootstocks; 18 inches high;

for bank-binding. Yellow flowers in summer.

Iberis sempervirens. Hardy candytuft. Evergreen. Sun to partial shade. Clumps of dark green leaves, 6-8 inches high, spreads apart with age to reveal woody stems. White flowers in spring. Tolerates drought.

Leiophyllum buxifolium. Sand-myrtle. Evergreen. Sun to light shade. Low, spreading shrub; 12 inches high. Can be grown from seed. Needs acid, humusy soil enriched with sand and peat moss.

Pachistima canbyi. Pachistima. Evergreen. Sun to shade. Woody spreading plant; 8-12 inches high. Small, dark green leaves. Prefers rich soil on the acid side. Sometimes slow to get established.

Teucrium chamaedrys. Germander. Evergreen. Sun to partial shade. Upright little bushes, 8-12 inches high. Dark green leaves.

Large Vines and Ramblers for Ground Cover

Akebia quinata. Five-leaf akebia. Deciduous. Sun. Woody vine to use as a ground cover; 12 inches high. Keep it away from trees and shrubs as it will gain hold on and twine around. Curious flowers not showy; but elegant foliage.

Lonicera japonica. Japanese honeysuckle. Semi-evergreen. Sun to partial shade. Fragrant flowers, white changing to yellow. For large banks and steep slopes. Stem-roots help bind soil, prevent erosion. When growth gets rampant, chop back ruthlessly in spring. **L. henryi** is less invasive, and tends to be evergreen.

Rosa. Rose. Climbers or ramblers of the **R. wichuraiana** type make excellent and tough ground covers. Deciduous. Sun. Trail on the ground, to 24 inches high. Some kinds form roots along the stems where they touch moist soil. Excellent bank-binder in large, sloping area.

Dwarf Needle-leaved Evergreens for Ground Cover

Juniperus (low-growing forms). Prostrate juniper. Sun. Spreading growth, 8-20 inches high. **J. horizontalis** has blue-green foliage; its cultivar **procumbens** is the creeping juniper, only a few inches high. Also excellent: **J. squamata, J. conferta** and **J. chinensis sargenti**, all with light-green or gray-green foliage.

Taxus (low-growing forms). Yew. Sun to partial shade. Spreading, about 12 inches high. Use **T. baccata repandens** (spreading English yew) or **T. canadensis stricta** (dwarf spreading Canada yew). All yews have very dark green needles.

Chapter 4
TREES FOR SHADE, FLOWERS AND DECORATIVE FRUIT

Every property needs at least one shade tree, more if there is room, and flowering trees too as space permits, but select no tree that is a maintenance trap. Avoid any tree known to be disease-prone (American elm), insect-ridden (black-locust), or having shallow wide-spreading roots (cottonwood). Also beware of trees with large, brittle branches that may snap in a wind storm (silver maple), kinds that send suckers far out into lawn and garden areas (some poplars), and any with smelly blossoms (female poplar, male ailanthus), or littering fruit (red mulberry).

When you plant a tree, you are planting shade, either dense as from a sycamore, or light and open, as from a honey-locust. You are also planting shape, background and color—from bark, leaves, flowers and possibly fruit.

Select trees for screening, to shut off an unsightly view, to afford privacy from neighbors, or to muffle street noise. Trees can mask or complement the stark lines of buildings. Trees along a street give a feeling of welcome.

To select the tree that will give maximum effect with minimum effort, consider: (1) reliable winter hardiness; (2) form suited to use; (3) mature size, including rate of growth; (4) any undesirable characteristics; and (5) availability.

1. Hardiness. This pertains to climate, soil, moisture, heat, and cold. For example, the European mountain-ash thrives in northern climates but is short-lived in the South. The ginkgo and the London plane-tree prosper even in air-polluted city gardens and along city streets. The sugar maple expires in cities; it needs fresh air. For easy maintenance, select trees known to thrive in your climate. Take a look at what is growing well on your neighbors' places. Obviously, some watering, feeding, pruning and spraying may be needed but not to the point of being a weekly or monthly chore.

2. Form Depends on Function. A broad-spreading shade tree, like the sugar maple, is fine in the open spaces of a park or large yard, but not along a driveway, or dripping branches over the front door. Slim upright trees, such as Lombardy poplar, are fine for screening or to line a drive, but one won't function well to shade an outdoor-living area, and it is certainly not a tree to nourish for ten years with the hope of eventually enjoying a picnic lunch beneath it.

Tree people say there are six basic shapes: *columnar* (Lombardy poplar), *oval* (horse-chestnut, red ash), *pyramidal* (pin oak, yellow-wood), *round* (catalpa, willow oak), *spreading/horizontal* (Amur cork-tree, weeping willow) and *vase* (hybrid elm). Sometimes a seventh category is suggested, *weeping* (willow). This sounds perfectly sensible on paper, but when you go to the nursery, the basic shapes may not be so obvious because specimens there are immature. Ask someone at the nursery or read catalog descriptions carefully for information about the two-dimensional shape of the tree you are considering.

3. Size is a consideration everyone takes seriously—at least at first. The temptation is to fall in love with an appealing young specimen at the nursery—like a St. Bernard puppy in a pet shop—and take it home, regardless of its expected size at maturity. That symmetrical Norway spruce at the nursery, only 6 feet tall, appears ideal for planting near the entry. But it will grow to 70 feet, with a spread of 40 feet.

When you plant two or more trees of the same kind, the general rule for spacing is at a distance equal to 75 percent of height. For example, trees expected to grow 20 feet tall should by planted 15 feet apart.

Also to be considered is a tree's expected growth rate under normal conditions. Sometimes a potentially large tree grows so slowly that it is still a good choice. For example, a tulip-tree may grow to 100 feet, but this takes a hundred years. You may elect to plant the tulip-tree for your own enjoyment and let future generations worry about its ultimate size. It takes a ginkgo fifteen to twenty years to make a real show.

Carefree Deciduous Trees for Shade

The heights given below merely indicate the average height in cultivation about 25 to 30 years after planting. Of course, individual specimens of the larger trees may continue to grow, under favorable conditions, for many decades and will reach 100 to 140 feet by the time your grandchildren are grown. Such are the bur oak, sugar maple, tulip-tree, white ash and white oak. Moderately quick-growing trees have one asterisk (*), and fast-growing trees have two (**).

American linden, *Tilia americana*, 50 ft., heavy shade, fragrant blossoms in late June, slow-growing.

American sycamore, *Platanus occidentalis*, 50 ft., heavy shade, often holds its leaves until fall, mottled bark, magnificent when large.**

Amur cork-tree, *Phellodendron amurense*, 40 ft., wide-spreading top, compound leaves, black berries, good in dry soils.*

Box-elder, *Acer negundo*, 40 ft., open airy growth, often several main trunks, very hardy.**

Buisman hybrid elm, *Ulmus* 'Christine Buisman,' 40 ft., resistant to Dutch elm disease.*

Bur oak, *Quercus macrocarpa*, 50 ft., needs space to develop superbly, slow-growing.

Chinese chestnut, *Castanea mollissima*, 50 ft., good shade, edible nuts after ten years, slow-growing.

Chinese elm, *see* Siberian elm.

Cutleaf weeping birch, *Betula pendula gracilis*, 40 ft., white bark, exotic look, light shade.*

European ash, *Fraxinus excelsior*, 50 ft., good shade.*

European beech, *Fagus sylvatica*, 50 ft., smooth pale-gray bark, low branches, glossy leaves.*

European birch, *Betula pendula*, 40 ft., white bark, very graceful; light shade.*

European hornbeam, *Carpinus betulus*, 50 ft., broad-pyramidal form, densely foliaged, slow-growing.

Ginkgo, *Ginkgo triloba*, 40 ft., stiff-looking and often odd-shaped when young, beautiful in 15 years, brassy late-autumn foliage, immune to all pests.

Green ash, *Fraxinus pennsylvanica lanceolata*, 50 ft., stately form, solid shade.**

Hackberry, *Celtis occidentalis*, 50 ft., elmlike leaves, branching crown, open shade.**

Horse-chestnut, *Aesculus hippocastanum*, 50 ft., large compound leaves, smooth bark, vigorous form with pendent limbs when mature, candelabra blossoms, dense shade.**

Kentucky coffee-tree, *Gymnocladus dioica*, 40 ft., rounded, open form, large leaves.*

Little-leaf linden, *Tilia cordata*, 40 ft., densely foliaged, graceful branches, fragrant flowers in June, heavy shade.*

Locust, *Robinia pseudoacacia*, 50 ft., high open form, cool blue-green foliage, limbs brittle when old (avoid planting near walks and drives).**

Lombardy poplar, *Populus nigra italica*, 50 ft., narrow-columned, short-lived. Leaves always in motion.**

Modesto ash, *Fraxinus velutina glauca*, 20 ft., rounded form, drought-resistant, good in small areas.**

Moraine locust, *Gleditsia triacanthos*, 50 ft., open, graceful, airy form, grass grows underneath, light shade.**

Norway maple, *Acer platanoides*, 50 ft., good shade and fall coloring.**

Pagoda-tree, *Sophora japonica*, 40 ft., spreading crown, delicate but dense foliage, clustered flowers in August on mature trees.*

Pin oak, *Quercus palustris*, 50 ft., densely foliaged, downward-slanted limbs, pyramidal effect.*

Red maple, *Acer rubrum*, 50 ft., small leaves for a maple but good shade, shallow rooting, leaves color in fall.**

Red oak, *Quercus borealis*, 40 ft., rounded form, crimson autumn color.*

River birch, *Betula nigra*, 50 ft., upright form with branching trunk, ragged bark.**

Russian olive, *Elaeagnus angustifolia*, 20 ft., silvery foliage, stands drought, very hardy.**

Sassafras, *Sassafras albidum*, 40 ft., irregular open form, interesting leaves color reddish in fall.*

Scarlet oak, *Quercus coccinea*, 40 ft., irregular form, brilliant autumn color, slow-growing.

Shagbark hickory, *Carya ovata*, 50 ft., rugged, picturesque form, many branched and tall-oval in form, bark smooth on young trees, shaggy-plated on older ones, needs care in transplanting and moist soil.**

Siberian elm, *Ulmus pumila*, 40 ft., spreading form, good autumn foliage. Very hardy.**

Sugar maple, *Acer saccharum*, 50 ft., dense crown of foliage turning orange, yellow and red in fall. Rather slow-growing, handsome.

Sweet gum, *Liquidambar styraciflua*, 50 ft., star-shaped leaves, wine-red autumn color, moist soil.*

Tulip-tree, *Liriodendron tulipifera*, 50 ft., tall straight trunk, beautiful leaves, orange-green flowers in June, yellow autumn color.**

Weeping willow, *Salix babylonica*, 40 ft., long pendent flexible branchlets, lower ones touching the ground.**

White ash, *Fraxinus americana*, 50 ft., large compound leaves, open growth, stately when fully grown.*

White oak, *Quercus alba*, 50 ft., spreading form, vigorous noble look, red leaves in fall, slow-growing.

Willow oak, *Quercus phellos*, 40 ft., slender, light-green leaves, more airy and open effect than other oaks, hardy to lower New England.*

Yellow-wood, *Cladrastis lutea*, 30 ft., low-branching.*

Carefree Flowering Trees

Very few showy flowering trees grow to more than 25 feet tall, and many are nearly as wide as high. In this list the specified heights are the ultimate height, which most will attain in fifteen to twenty years. Exceptions are the empress-tree, which may take longer to reach 40 feet and may then, in a fortunate situation, go on well beyond that; and the saucer magnolia, which may develop into a fairly large tree in time. Many flowering trees, also, branch fairly close to the ground, and have the effect of large shrubs, so that they can be used in combinations, where there is space, or as isolated specimens.

American redbud, *Cercis canadensis*, 15 ft. Pink pea-flowers all along branches in May.

Bechtel's crab apple, *Malus ioensis plena*, 20 ft. Double pale-pink flowers in profusion in May.

Empress-tree, *Pawlownia tomentosa*, 40 ft. Hardy to lower New York State. Large panicles of violet flowers before the leaves.

English hawthorn, *Crataegus oxyacantha*, 15 ft. White fragrant flowers in large clusters. Scarlet berries. Also a pink-flowered form.

European mountain-ash, *Sorbus aucuparia*, 25 ft. White flowers in spring. Red berries in summer and fall.

Flowering cherries, *Prunus serrulata*, 20 ft. Wealth of fragrant white flowers just before the leaves. A fine variety is known as *P. sargentii*.
   Prunus sieboldii, 25 ft. Dangling clusters of pink flowers. A fine lawn specimen.
   Prunus subhirtella pendula, 25 ft. Fountain of pink flow-

ers in spring.

Prunus yedoensis, 30 ft. Fast-growing, single white or palest pink flowers.

Flowering dogwood, *Cornus florida*, 30 ft. Familiar, and one of the outstanding American trees.

Flowering peach, *Prunus persica* varieties, 10 ft. White, pink or red flowers in May.

Flowering plum, *Prunus blireiana*, 20 ft. Rose-colored double flowers in May, purple-tinged leaves.

Prunus pissardi, 20 ft. Deep-pink flowers, plum-colored leaves. Also a white-flowered form.

Franklinia, *Gordonia alatamaha*, 20 ft. Hardy to Massachusetts. Large white flowers in autumn.

Fringe-tree, *Chionanthus virginica*, 20 ft. Hardy to lower New York State.

Goldenchain, *Laburnum vossei*, 25 ft. Pendent racems of yellow pea-flowers in May.

Goldenrain-tree, *Koelreuteria paniculata*, 30 ft. Panicles of bloom in midsummer.

Hopa crab apple, *Malus hopa*, 25 ft. Spectacular show of brilliant pink flowers in May.

Japanese crab apple, *Malus sieboldii*, 15 ft. Slender habit, blush-pink flowers.

Malus floribunda, 20 ft. Buds carmine, opening to pink flowers, then white. Very showy.

Japanese dogwood, *Cornus kousa*, 20 ft. Blooms later than flowering dogwood. Leaves scarlet in autumn.

Mimosa, *see* Silk-tree.

Red horse-chestnut, *Aesculus carnea*, 40 ft. Flowers flesh-colored to scarlet in June.

Sargent's crab apple, *Malus sargentii*, 6 ft. Shrublike; white flowers, red fruits.

Saucer magnolia, *Magnolia soulangeana*, 30 ft. White, pink and rose-colored flowers in different varieties.

Shadblow, *Amelanchier grandiflora*, 25 ft. White flowers in May. Fruits yellow or red.

Siberian crab apple, *Malus baccata*, 25 ft. White flowers in May. Fruits yellow or red.

Silk-tree, *Albizia julibrissin*, 30 ft. Airy foliage. Pink flowers like erect tassels in summer. May winterkill north of Philadelphia.

Silverbell, *Halesia monticola*, 30 ft. Profuse white flowers in late May. Rich moist soil.

Star magnolia, *Magnolia stellata*, 15 ft. White flowers in early spring.

Tree lilac, *Syringa japonica*, 25 ft. Large trusses of white flowers in June. Wide-branching.

Washington hawthorn, *Crataegus cordata*, 20 ft. Flowers in late spring. Fall berries. Leaves turn red in autumn. There are other fine species and hybrids of crab apples, cherries, hawthorns and plums. Consult the catalogs of leading nurseries. In the northernmost parts of the country the crab apples are hardier than the cherries and plums.

Carefree Evergreen Trees

American arborvitae, *Thuja occidentalis*, to 60 ft. but many much lower-growing forms of various shapes. Dense foliage, scale-like leaves. Slow growing.

American holly, *Ilex opaca*, to 40 ft. Familiar glossy leaves. Male and female trees needed to produce berries. May require spraying for leaf miners.

Austrian pine, *Pinus nigra*, to 60 ft. Dark needles, open growth. Fine for background. Hardy.

Black Hills spruce, *Picea glauca densata*, to 40 ft. Slow-growing, compact, symmetrical.

Cedar of Lebanon, *Cedrus libani*, to 60 ft. Blue-green foliage. Not hardy north of New York City except along the coast.

Colorado spruce, *Picea pungens*, to 40 ft. Blue-green foliage. Many varieties, very hardy.

Douglas-fir, *Pseudotsuga taxifolia*, to 40 ft. (eventually a giant in nature). Variety *glauca* is the best in northern and eastern gardens.

Eastern hemlock, *Tsuga canadensis*, to 60 ft. Graceful, soft-foliaged. Needs lime soil.

English holly, *Ilex aquifolium*, 20 ft. Perhaps more beautiful than American holly, but not reliably hardy north of Philadelphia. Slow-growing. May require spraying for leaf miners.

Hinoki false-cypress, *Chamaecyparis obtusa*, to 20 ft. Foliage flat and frondlike, drooping. Many varieties.

Norway or red pine, *Pinus resinosa*, 60 ft. One of the hardiest and best large pines. Open, branching shape.

Norway spruce, *Picea abies*, to 40 ft. Many forms. Generally dense, pyramidal, light-green foliage effect. Pendent cones.

Scotch pine, *Pinus sylvestris*, to 30 ft. Blue-green foliage. Picturesque habit.

White or Colorado fir, *Abies concolor*, to 40 ft. Many forms. Soft-green color effect.

White pine, *Pinus strobus*, to 60 ft. Majestic tree, branches beautifully spaced. When older, dark foliage.

4. Undesirable Traits Vary in Importance. Some make a tree completely undesirable for planting; others may be tolerable. The American elm is at present a poor choice. Thornless honey-locust is subject to attack by the mimosa webworm—as is the mimosa (silk-tree) itself—and this needs annual spraying. Mulberry species and the female ginkgo have objectionable fruit; plant the fruitless variety of white mulberry and male ginkgo. More tolerable are the traits of oaks, hickories, horse-chestnuts and crab apples that drop fruit over lawn or terrace—fruits attractive to children who are always tempted to use them as missiles. The stickery-sphere seed pods dropped on the lawn by sweet gum are a nuisance, but easily managed by an annual rake-up in the spring and completely offset by the glorious coloration of the autumn foliage.

Poplars, silk-trees, maples and elms readily seed into lawns and flower beds. But this is really no problem unless the seedlings are allowed to grow for a season or two; then they are hard to uproot and a real time-consumer. Some trees have hungry surface roots that rob the soil of all moisture, making it impossible to grow a decent lawn there, or flowers: maples, for example. Roots also may crack nearby pavement. Some trees have vigorous roots that seek out sewer lines and clog them—red and silver maples, elms and willows.

5. Availability. Narrow your list. Decide exactly what tree is your choice—and the best tree for the location. Then go after it. If it is not available at a local nursery, shop by mail. There is no reason to accept any substitute, unless you can honestly say that after further consideration it is in reality a better choice.

Planting Trees

If you have selected the right trees and planned for them in your design, minimum upkeep should be your reward. Before you rush out with the loaf of bread and jug of wine, take time to plant them properly.

The one major rule about tree planting is to dig a large hole. If the tree is balled and burlapped, dig a hole 2 feet wider than the rootball. Depth—check ring around the trunk to determine the original soil line—and plant to the same level.

If the soil is poor, dig an even wider and deeper hole, replacing a quantity of poor soil with the best possible topsoil.

Before adding soil around the rootball, add stakes or guy post. If the trunk is less than 3 inches in diameter, use one or two 6-foot poles set vertically next to the rootball. Fasten the trunk to the poles with loops of wire enclosed in a section of garden hose (to protect bark). For a trunk larger than 3 inches in diameter, use three guy wires, hose-covered, around the trunk about halfway up. Stake one guy wire to the ground in the direction of the prevailing wind, the other two placed to form an equilateral triangle.

After the stakes or guy wires are in place, fill in topsoil, being sure tree is positioned in a straight vertical position. Water well. After soil settles, add more to level off. Wrap trunk with burlap or creped kraft paper to prevent sunscald. Start wrapping at top; work down. Tie with stout cord, knotting about every 18 inches. Remove after two years, or when it begins to fall away.

How to compensate if you planted a tree without digging a large hole to begin with? You will have to water more frequently, in combination with more fertilizer, than for a tree well-planted to begin with. Soil that is heavily compacted is often either so dry that roots cannot prosper in it, or so poorly drained that water stands and suffocates the roots. If dryness is the problem, make a basin around the trunk that will hold water and fill it often to keep the soil evenly moist. A bubbler-soaker is excellent for this purpose. If the soil is too wet, gently mound it higher at the trunk than the surrounding area so that rain will run off from the tree, not be caught and held around it.

Trees Need Fertilizer

Feeding at the right time in the right amounts will give you healthy, strong trees that grow at a satisfying rate. Once a year is sufficient. If you start a new tree with a large hole and fill around it with good topsoil, no feeding will be needed the first year. After that, feed annually, in spring. Measure the trunk 3 feet above ground. Allow 2 pounds of 5-10-5 for each inch of diameter. A one-pound coffee can holds about 2 pounds of fertilizer. Use soil auger, crowbar, or posthole digger. Make holes 15 to 24 inches deep and 18 to 24 inches apart around dripline of the tree (this is the area underneath the longest branches). Distribute fertilizer equally in the holes. Fill back up with soil made by mixing equal parts soil and sand; this accepts moisture readily. You can apply a foliar plant food to the leaves by using a hose-end or pressure sprayer.

Trees should be deeply watered frequently during the first two seasons after planting. An automatic watering system will help here. Once established, trees can survive long periods of drought. City trees get very little water because large paved areas are so planned that moisture drains away quickly before it can seep underneath. They adjust. Lawn trees compete with grass and other plants nearby. At first, it is necessary to let water soak slowly for several hours around each tree, ideally using a Melnor bubbler-soaker attachment. Later, in times of severe drought, if there is a water shortage, water the trees first; then choice shrubbery; last of all herbaceous flowers which by comparison in the final analysis are expendable. It takes years to grow a tree; only a season or two to grow a flower garden.

Mulching helps conserve moisture around a tree and reduces maintenance—no need to hand trim after mowing the grass and no danger of scruffing the bark with passes from the mower. Both points are important. Trees are naturally mulched in the forest by layers of leaves that fall and lie year after year gradually decomposing. Not possible in cultivated areas. So, add a mulch of pine bark, tanbark, ground corncobs, redwood bark chips, peanut hulls or pebbles. General rule: Area to mulch beneath a tree should be twelve times diameter of the trunk. A tree 1 inch in diameter will need mulch a foot in diameter. A tree with a 5-inch trunk will need a mulch area 5 feet in diameter.

Pruning is routine. If you have chosen the right tree, it is also minimal. Winter is a good time to check overall structure. After leafing-out of tree, it is easier to find dead, dying or unsightly parts. Pruning will help improve the appearance. Direct the growth and avoid major surgery later. Once-a-year pruning will make it easy to get rid of undesirable branches and shoots while they are still small—no sawing, only simple cutting with a pair of shears.

When pruning is in order, look for: dead, dying or unsightly tree parts. Sprouts growing at or near base of trunk. Branches growing toward center of tree. Crossed branches. (Crossed branches rub together; disease and decay fungi enter through abraded parts.) V crotches: If possible remove one branch; v's split easily in wind, ice and snow storms. Multiple leaders: If tree should have one to develop typical shape, remove all but one leader. Nuisance growth: Remove branches headed toward utility wires. That block view of street (potential traffic hazard, for example). That may screen a desirable view. Remove branches that stop breezes. Remove lower limbs that shade lawn too much or make walking underneath hazardous.

When you prune, don't leave stubs. They die back, tend to rot, and become a breeding place for dangerous fungi. Small cuts heal quickly. Large cuts—anything more than 1 inch in diameter—need treatment with antiseptic tree dressing to prevent the entrance of decay-disease while wound heals.

Chapter 5

SHRUBS AND VINES FOR COLOR ALL YEAR

Plant shrubs wherever you want year-round interest—flowers, foliage, berries and colorful bark—and no demanding upkeep. Evergreen and deciduous shrubs come in all sizes and shapes for plantings in sun and shade, in moist or dry soil, and in all climates. Depend on them for screening, dense and impenetrable or filtered and illusionary, and for hedging, low and formal or tall and billowy.

With shrubs, there is no need to have a maintenance problem. Apply a thick mulch around them to avoid weeding and cultivating. If you can't prune and trim annually, try for once every other year.

A common mistake with shrubs is to plant one in a space that is too small. Multiply this by planting a whole bed of shrubs poorly scaled to the space, and you will have a problem that grows worse every year. More and more pruning will be needed, until finally you give in and let the shrubbery take over, literally blocking out the doors and windows of your home.

Another maintenance trap with shrubs is to spot them all around the lawn and garden, thus necessitating additional trimming, and tedious mowing around. Better to group shrubs—even if you have only a few—in complete and well-designed beds than to scatter them all over the yard.

Different kinds of shrubs can be interplanted in a pleasing way so that foliage blends or contrasts, textures complement, and flowers come in and out of bloom in an ever-changing picture. Another approach is to mass shrubs of one kind, lilacs for example. Within this planting there will be early-, mid-season- and late-blooming varieties. The same can be done with rhododendrons and azaleas.

Shrubs for All Seasons

If it is important that you have flowers over a long season, with plenty to cut for bouquets, especially some with long stems for large arrangements, flowering shrubs are the answer. Your display can start with witch-hazels that bloom in the first spring weather—which may come in a January thaw in your area—and finish with witch-hazels that bloom in October and November. For fall and winter there are many shrubs with bright berries, and the red-twig dogwood has colorful bark that is spectacular against new-fallen snow.

For entrance plantings on close view around the year, evergreens are the obvious choice. Selected with care, tailored and neat, these will prove a constant joy. To avoid maintenance, clearly delineate the bed design with a brick mowing strip or a retaining wall. Mulch the surface with wood chips or pebbles. This kind of reserve keeps the entry area looking well-groomed with little or no upkeep. For seasonal flowers, use a few well-placed containers.

Shrubs properly planted and at the right time require the least maintenance. Plan first. If you wait to decide what you want until you go to a local nursery, you will likely be tempted to buy some of everything that appeals to you. If the assortment turns into a low-upkeep planting at home, you will have worked a modern-day miracle. The miracle happens only when you plan it carefully. And this is a great pastime for winter—or a relaxed summer day when you can spread your catalogs and papers on a shaded table under a tree, or maybe in an air-conditioned room. The idea is to do the planning when planting time is yet to be. Try to locate the right shrubs in the right place at the beginning. If you have to move a shrub later to a better position, don't hesitate to transplant, but it's work you should try to avoid.

Shrubs are available at local garden centers as container-grown plants (usually in cans or plastic pots), large specimens sometimes balled-and-burlapped, and early in spring there may be bare-root deciduous varieties. By mail most shrubs come bare-root only in early spring for immediate planting. More and more shrubs are displayed in garden centers as container-grown plants that can be seen and selected—and planted—any time the weather lets you work outdoors. This permits landscape work to proceed over a long season, instead of being limited to a few too-short weeks in spring, and again for a too-short period in early fall.

The lists below first group deciduous shrubs according to

flowering season, with mature heights specified, followed by a selection of kinds for berries, and finally plants to consider among the broadleaf and needle-leaf evergreens. From these lists, you will see that the range of choice is wide in all types and sizes. You can get an initial acquaintance with any of them in nursery catalogs, but the better way is to see them personally in a nursery, arboretum or in neighbors' gardens.

Easy Deciduous Flowering Shrubs

EARLY SPRING

Cornelian-cherry, *Cornus mas*, 15 ft.
Flowering quince, *Chaenomeles lagenaria*, 3 to 8 ft.
Forsythia, *Forsythia spectabilis* and hybrids, 10 ft.
Pussy willow, *Salix discolor* and *S. viminalis*, 20 ft.

MID-SPRING

Azalea, *Azalea mollis* strain, many hybrids, 2 to 5 ft.
Bridal-wreath, *Spiraea prunifolia*, 6 ft.
Bush honeysuckle, *Lonicera tatarica*, 8 ft.
Deutzia, various hybrids, 3 ft.
Flowering almond, *Prunus glandulosa*, 4 ft.
French lilac, *Syringa lemoinei* hybrids, 8 to 12 ft.
Jetbead, *Rhodotypos tetrapetala*, 5 ft.
Persian lilac, *Syringa persica*, 6 ft.
Van Houtte's spirea, *Spiraea vanhouttei*, 6 ft.

LATE SPRING

Beauty-bush, *Kolkwitzia amabilis*, 8 ft.
Double-file viburnum, *Viburnum tomentosum mariesi*, 7 ft.
Fragrant snowball, *Viburnum carlcephalum*, 6 ft.
Japanese snowball, *Viburnum tomentosum sterile*, 10 ft.
Kerria, *Kerria japonica pleniflora*, 8 ft.
Mock-orange, *Philadelphus* species and varieties, 10 ft.

Red spirea, *Spiraea japonica coccinea*, 3 ft.
Strawberry-shrub, *Calycanthus floridus*, 6 ft.
Weigela, *Weigela florida* and hybrids, 8 ft.

MIDSUMMER

Abelia, *Abelia grandiflora*, 4 ft.
Beauty-berry, *Callicarpa giraldiana*, 8 ft.
Buddleia, *Buddleia davidi* and hybrids, 8 ft.
French tamarix, *Tamarix gallica* and hybrids, 8 ft. Hardy to
    southern New England.
Hypericum, *Hypericum Hidcote*, 3 ft., lower in cold areas.
Potentilla, *Potentilla fruticosa*, 2 ft.
Smoke-tree, *Cotinus coggygria*, 12 ft.

LATE SUMMER-EARLY FALL

Blue-mist flower, *Caryopteris mastacanthus*, 3 ft. Often dies
    to the ground in North, but comes up every spring.
Chaste-tree, *Vitex agnus-castus*, 10 ft.
Peegee hydrangea, *Hydrangea paniculata grandiflora*, 10 ft.
Rose-of-Sharon, *Hibiscus syriacus*, 8 ft.

SHRUBS AND LOW TREES WITH FALL
AND WINTER BERRIES

Barberries	Hawthorns
Beauty-berry	Holly
Cornelian-cherry	Jetbead
Cotoneasters	Mountain-ash
Crab apples	Rugosa roses
Dogwood (also the red-twig dogwood for winter bark)	Snowberry
	Viburnums

DWARF BROADLEAF EVERGREENS
(under 4 feet)

Andromeda, *Pieris floribunda.*

Barberry, *Berberis julianae* and *B. mentorensis* hold their leaves until mid-winter. Other evergreen kinds not reliably hardy north of Washington, D.C.

Boxwood, littleleaf, *Buxus microphylla.* Hardy to lower New York and Connecticut.

Euonymus, *Euonymus fortunei vegetus.*

Holly-grape, *Mahonia aquifolium.*

Holly, short-leaved, *Ilex convexa.*

Leucothoe, drooping, *Leucothoe catesbaei.* North of New York City, best in sheltered situation.

Rhododendron, *Rhododendron carolinianum.*

Rock-spray, *Cotoneaster divaricata* and *C. horizontalis*, low, trailing.

MEDIUM-HEIGHT BROADLEAF EVERGREENS
(5 to 10 feet)

Andromeda, *Pieris japonica.*

Euonymus, *Euonymus patens*, hardy in New England. *E. japonicus* larger, hardy to Philadelphia.

Firethorn, *Pyracantha coccinea lalandi.*

Holly, inkberry, *Ilex glabra.*

Mountain-laurel, *Kalmia latifolia.*

Rhododendron, *Rhododendron maximum*, *R. catawbiense* and hybrids. Note: The evergreen azaleas, *Rhododendron obtusum* and varieties are hardy only in the South.

DWARF NEEDLE EVERGREENS
(mostly under 5 feet)

Arborvitae, globe, *Thuja occidentalis globosa* and other dwarf forms.

Juniper, many forms of *Juniperus*, low and spreading, often beautifully colored and textured; silvery or blue-green in summer, purple-bronze in winter. Notably *J. chinensis hetzi, J. horizontalis plumosa, J. pfitzeriana* and *J. sabina*. Taller forms, upright or rounded, are *J.c. keteleeri, J.c. pyramidalis* and *J. scopulorum*.

Pine, Mugho, *Pinus mugo*, compact, broad-bushy, dark.

Yew, *Taxus media*, various horticultural forms, and *T. cuspidata nana*, wide-spreading, low.

HEDGES

Shrubs provide the material for hedges, no matter how formal or informal. For low upkeep, choose a slow-growing hedge that will need clipping only once a year, maybe only once every two or three years. It is easy with a fast-growing hedge to become a slave—once a month you give the weekend to trimming your hedge. If you do any hedge pruning, remember to keep the plants wider at the base than at the top. This lets light in to the lowest growth on the hedge—and keeps it lively and full there. Flowering shrubs like forsythia, lilac or weigela used for hedging should never be clipped into formal shapes.

SHRUBS FOR LOW, CLIPPED HEDGES
(3 feet high or less)

Barberry, *Berberis* species and varieties, especially *B. thunbergi* and its dwarf red variety.

Box, Korean, *Buxus microphylla koreana*, low-growing, slow.

Currant, Alpine, *Ribes alpinus*, dense, very hardy.

Euonymus, *Euonymus fortunei vegetus* and *E. patens*.

Holly, short-leaved, *Ilex convexa*.

Ninebark, *Physocarpus opulifolius nanus*.

Pachistima, *Pachistima canbyi*, beautiful edging plant, under 1 foot.

Privet, Amur, *Ligustrum amurense*, very hardy and tough.

Privet, Regel's, *Ligustrum obtusifolium regelianum*, graceful, branching.

Viburnum, *Viburnum opulus nanum*, fine for moist, heavy soil.

SHRUBS FOR MEDIUM TO TALL CLIPPED HEDGES
(4 to 8 feet high)

Arborvitae, *Arborvitae occidentalis*, evergreen.
Buckthorn, *Rhamnus cathartica*, withstands drought.
Hemlock, *Tsuga canadensis*, evergreen.
Juniper, *Juniperus chinensis keteleeri*, evergreen.
Rock-spray, *Cotoneaster acutifolia* and *C. divaricata*.
Spruce, Colorado, *Picea pungens*, blue-green, evergreen.
Yew, *Taxus media hicksi* and *T.m. hatfieldi*, the latter more
  spreading. Evergreen.

SHRUBS FOR UNCLIPPED HEDGES

Almost any shrub, deciduous or evergreen, can be used in quantity, unclipped, to make an effective and sizable hedge. But sooner or later some judicious pruning will be needed to keep it from becoming an overgrown and overwhelming boundary, out of proportion, in all likelihood, to the rest of the garden. Dead wood and *old* wood should be removed on forsythia, hibiscus, lilacs, mock-orange, viburnums and others. Suckers at the base will have to be kept down. Privet, allowed to grow naturally, can make a fine background in time but tends to become top heavy. And some flowering shrubs—mock-orange for one—may at times need entirely too much spraying against black aphids. Shrubs which do not grow too high are the most manageable, and when in bloom show themselves off at eye-level. Here are some of the best low-maintenance ones:

Beauty-bush, *Kolkwitzia amabilis*, to 7 ft. Arching branches
  almost to the ground, pink flowers in late spring.
Burning-bush, *Euonymus alatus*, to 5 ft. Blazing autumn col-
  or. Also a dwarf form.
Flowering quince, *Chaenomeles* hybrids (often sold as *Cydo-
  nia*), to 6 ft. or kept down to 3 or 4 ft. Early spring bloom,
  white, pink or red. Very hardy.
Forsythia, *Forsythia* Lynwood Gold, to 6 ft.
Honeysuckle, *Lonicera tatarica*, 6 ft. Rose-pink flowers in

spring. Charming small leaves.

Lilac, *Syringa sweginflexa*, to 5 ft. Tidy habit, long trusses of pink flowers in late May. Also selected named hybrids of other lilac species.

Rose, *Rosa polyantha*, 1 to 1 1/2 ft., blooming all summer.

Rose, *Rosa rugosa*, excellent foliage, thorny barrier, wild-rose-type flowers all summer, brilliant orange-red autumn fruits, called rose hips.

Sweet pepper-bush, *Clethra alnifolia*, to 5 ft. Spikes of fragrant white flowers in August, good foliage. Also a pink variety, *rosea*, lower-growing. Both good in moist soil.

Viburnum, *Viburnum opulus nanum*, to 2 ft. Dense, vigorous, very hardy. Flowers inconspicuous. Will thrive in heavy moist soil.

Weigela modern hybrids, 5 to 6 ft. Variety Majesteux 3 to 4 ft. White, pink or red flowers in late May and June.

Vines for Flowers and Foliage

Vines serve several purposes. Where a tree or tall shrub is impractical, they reach their greenery and blossoms high into the air, making a wall of shade and privacy. Trained against the stark walls of contemporary architecture, they soften its severity without taking too much space. Valuable for their rich texture and interesting leaf patterns are favorites such as the silver lace vine, Dutchman's-pipe, ampelopsis, English ivy in its countless varieties and Boston ivy.

Silver lace vine and kudzu are among the fastest growers, but like many vines, must be kept in bounds or they will take over. Many vines produce beautiful flowers—among them clematis, rambler roses, wisteria, trumpet vine, some honeysuckles, climbing hydrangea, bougainvillea (in the South), passion flower and winter jasmine. Among the best of the evergreen vines are wintercreeper (a climbing euonymus), evergreen types of clematis and hardy English ivies.

Large-flowered clematis, the most colorful of vines, are outstanding grown on trellises, arbors, pergolas, wall corners or trained to tumble over walls. Many varieties are hardy in cold climates and will bloom year after year if provided with rich soil (on the alkaline side of the pH scale) and half a day or more of sunlight. Ideally, the roots should be shaded with most of the stems and leaves in sun.

Shrubs for the Birds

Brilliant fall berries that brighten the landscape and attract birds during the cold months appear on many of the flowering shrubs. Berries of the Wright viburnum are borne in clusters of vivid, shining red. Some viburnums, *V. setigerum* for example, bear golden or orange fruit. Among other berried shrubs popular with birds are choke-cherry, Milky Way dogwood, cotoneaster, pyracantha and winterberry. Still others include Sargent crab apple, serviceberry (shadblow), arbutus, bearberry, bayberry, coral ardisia (in the South), Japanese aucuba (hardy to New York City), many barberries, dogwoods, corkbush varieties, honeysuckle, the blueberries and other edible-berried shrubs and most of the flowering fruit trees.

The Rose, Perfection Among Flowers

Anyone can grow roses, it's true, but only in a place that receives a few hours of direct sunlight. Even if your space is limited to a sunny window ledge, a window box, or a fire escape, you can grow pots of miniature roses if you are absolutely faithful with the watering can; don't ever let them dry out severely.

Roses make the best show when they are massed in the garden—and even better when the same colors or varieties are planted together. Rosarians have complicated recipes for soil preparation, but unless you're going into rose-show competitions, decent roses will grow in almost any soil. Just dig a big, generous hole that allows the roots to spread out comfortably at planting time.

In the absence of plentiful rains, water slowly and deeply once a week, placing the hose nozzle on the ground; sprinkling the foliage only spreads disease.

Tree roses are the result of sophisticated grafting techniques by specialists. In windy areas tree roses need a stake to keep them from whipping. Where winter temperatures drop below 10 degrees F., tree roses have to be carefully dug and buried in trenches, or else treated as annuals and replaced every spring.

Seafoam is a small-flowered but everblooming rose that grows exceptionally well in large pots or tubs—for decorating a porch or other outdoor living area. Container roses need abundant feeding and watering—and usually a pot or tub with a minimum diameter of 15 inches and similar depth.

Heirloom, with its luscious pink flowers, and Golden Gate, are typical of today's hybrid roses—strong-growing, innately vigorous, and everblooming—from the first flowers of June until autumn frost. Shrub roses, especially hybrids of *Rosa rugosa*, are great to grow by the sea.

The Keys to Healthy Shrubs and Vines

Plants can live for a long time without plant food, but only the desert plants designed by nature to do so can live for very long without water.

Water is especially important when new plants are set, and depending on the size of the shrubs (which governs the amount of water lost through foliage hourly) it remains absolutely vital the first and even second season.

Once your shrub is in its planting hole, add the equivalent of a bucket of water daily for the first three or four weeks for medium-large plants, and two for small trees and very large shrubs. Water twice weekly after that throughout the first season and once a week the second season for large shrubs.

Mulches piled over the root system area of new plantings help preserve moisture and keep high summer temperatures from searing the new root growth your shrub is putting out in order to establish itself in its new home. Use acid mulches, such as oak leaves or Canadian peat moss, for plants, particularly the evergreens, that require acid soils. Use spoiled hay, plastic mulch strips, fallen leaves of less acid-reacting trees—for plants that prefer soils on the alkaline side, lilacs for example. Wood ashes make a good mulch for lilacs in the spring.

As a rule of thumb, newly set plants should not require more fertilizer than that incorporated into the planting soil in which they are set. The second season, or whenever they begin to put forth vigorous new growth, additional fertilizer may be employed. Thereafter, the shrubs should be fed just before and just when they are starting to make new growth, generally early or mid-spring. Additional fast-acting fertilizer may be added, as necessary, up to about August 1 in the North, September 1 in the deep South. Slow-release fertilizers, such as bone meal, can be applied to all types of shrubs and vines in fall and winter.

To fertilize shrubbery borders, scatter a handful of the fertilizer in a ring around the plant, with more toward the outward edge of the ring. The ring should not go beyond the drip line of the outer leaves. You can also apply foliar fertilizer with a hose-end or pressure sprayer during the active growing season.

Bouquets from Shrubs

Bouquets of branches in bloom will last indoors longer if you follow these simple rules: Select stems laden with buds and with only a few opened flowers. Blossoms as open as you might enjoy them outdoors usually have been pollinated already and are ready to drop petals and form fruit. Cut, they'll last perhaps only a few hours. Unpollinated buds will open indoors and since pollination is not likely to occur, they'll stay lovely for days.

Plan your raid on the shrubbery border in the late afternoon and take with you a bucket filled with lukewarm water. Plunge the stems into the water as soon as they are cut and place the bucket in a shady, draft-free spot for several hours to allow the plant's cells to thoroughly fill with water. Slash the stems from the bottom up 3 or 4 inches to improve water intake. When you are ready to make up your bouquet, strip away leaves that will be below the waterline in your vase, add a cut flower food if you have it, and set the branches in a large, deep vase filled with cool, clean water.

Forcing Shrub Flowers Out of Season

The flower you'll see in spring is already formed within its bud in winter and in many shrubs can be easily forced to bloom well ahead of the natural season. Forsythia, flowering quince, pussy willow and spireas are among the most successful forced flowers. Choose subjects to be forced according to the shrub's normal blooming time. The earliest bloomers are those to force first; for instance, witch-hazel and forsythia. Cut on a warm winter day, and leave overnight in a bathtub half full of tepid water. Peel bark from stems 3 inches from bottom and place in a deep container full of tepid water. Set in a cool, dark, humid place. If your house is warm and dry everywhere, wrap newspapers around the branches and leave for three or four days. When the buds show a swelling, place the stems in a vase and arrange in a window where there is good light, but not a drying noonday spell of hot sunlight.

Many berries last on their branches through winter, and these are usually ideal subjects for drying. Preserving them for use in winter bouquets is extremely simple: Cut the branches (remembering that you are pruning your bush and improving its shape) when berries are at their brightest. Hang tied loosely together upside down in a cool, very dry place. In a week to ten days the branches will have dried and may be used to make lasting winter arrangements, possibly in combination with everlasting flowers you have dried from your garden, plus dried seedpods and plumes of grass gathered from fields or roadsides.

Chapter 6

FLOWERS FOR INDOOR/OUTDOOR BEAUTY

Grow the flowers you and your family like best and put the rest of your land in grass, ground cover, paving or under a deep mulch. Gather your flower forces in one mass. Concentrate effort. Save time in areas not important to you. Spend it where returns are highest. Work with a plan. In flower beds, keep the combinations simple. Try to achieve the results you want with just a few different flowers, and by making only one major planting in the spring (annuals) and sometimes one in autumn (hardy bulbs that will bloom in the spring).

Easy Ways with Annuals

Pick up started annual plants in spring at your local garden center on a day that is convenient for setting them out. All you have to do to keep annuals prospering and blooming is to cut off spent blooms before seeds ripen. Biologically all an annual wants to do is to flower, ripen seeds, then die. As long as you keep seeds from ripening, the plant keeps producing blooms in its natural urge to reproduce.

Before you go away on a summer trip, shear back annuals sufficiently to remove most of the current bloom. When you return in a week or two, the plants will be coming into new bloom—much nicer than coming home to a lot of seedy looking plants.

One way to use annuals with great style is to mass a single kind—a bed of Zenith zinnias, for example. Or mass in a monochromatic color scheme. You might put in a bed of Pink Cascade petunia, combined with Cherry Sundae giant hybrid zinnia, Pink Heather sweet-alyssum and other pink-flowered varieties of annuals such as baby's-breath, larkspur, snapdragons, stock, China-aster, verbena, phlox and Sensation cosmos.

Another pleasing way to use annual flowers is to develop a scheme providing one strong main color, maybe it will be yellow (marigolds, Gloriosa daisies and zinnias), a secondary complementary color, probably blue-to-lavender (ageratum and larkspur) and a dash of a third strong color for sharp accent—maybe it will be scarlet salvia.

In a shrubbery border there are always places to make pockets of annuals—most kinds grow in the sun. In shade you can use torenia, browallia, impatiens and semperflorens or wax begonias. Just prepare the soil 8 inches deep. If it is sticky clay or otherwise hard and not easy to dig, add a bale of sphagnum peat moss to every 200 square feet. Plant, water and mulch. That is all you have to do for all-season flowers.

If there is a patch of ground even 10 x 10 feet to spare, put in a little-upkeep cutting garden—row on row of annuals from seed packets or from young plants sold at nurseries or wayside stands. Maybe some corms of miniature gladiolus (these are better for cutting than the giant kinds that tend to stalkiness). Mulch deeply early in the season. Little or no weeding or watering will then be needed. Sounds too good to be true, but all you do, excepting initial planting, mulching and mixing 5-10-5 fertilizer into the top inch or two of soil, is to keep the flowers cut, having bouquets all over the house and plenty to spare for friends. You can even put down a systematic, timed-release fertilizer early in the season before planting that will feed constantly all season. Select annual flowers for a cutting garden in colors suited to the interior scheme of your home. All shades and hues are available. Here are favorite kinds for cutting:

Ageratum	Dahlia	Snapdragon
Baby's-breath	Larkspur	Stock
Calendula	Marigold	Verbena
Cornflower	Petunia	Zinnia
Cosmos	Salvia	

Color without Pain. In a shrubbery or herbaceous perennial border, where the soil has been worked into a friable condition, broadcast seeds of Iceland poppies, California poppies, larkspur and bachelor's-buttons on Christmas, New Year's or any other winter day—preferably when there is snow on the ground. These seeds of hardy annuals will nestle into the soil to germinate in the first warm days of spring. The young plants develop with vigor through cool nights and warm days, and produce blooms at the very beginning of the annual-flower season—actually by the time spring bulbs are finishing. When the earliest finishes, the hot-summer annuals like petunias and zinnias will be coming into bloom. This idea works best when seeds are sown over cultivated soil; obviously, fewer seeds will survive if they are sown in an area of unprepared soil, for example, an open meadow.

Container Gardening. Pots, tubs, planters and baskets of movable color can be enjoyed all spring, summer and fall around the garden—wherever you want flowers for a zing effect—up close or as a focal point for a vista. By the terrace or other outdoor living area. By the pool. At the entry. All you have to do for container-grown plants is to keep the soil moist and feed every other week. There is no stooping to weed, only an occasional minute to trim off spent blooms. This way a few flowering plants give you maximum effect for the least amount of trouble. Put them exactly where you want color at any given moment.

Disposable Garden Gloves

Groupings of container plants are more easily cared for, and make a greater show than single pots or tubs scattered around. Also, try repetition of the same plant in the same size pot. This modular look is appropriate with contemporary architecture; for example, nine 10-inch clay tubs of dwarf French marigolds, all of the same color, spaced out evenly in rows, three by three.

CONTAINER PLANTS
(except where noted, buy well-started plants)

For Sun	For Shade	For Hot, Dry Site
African daisy	Achimenes	Crassula
Ageratum	*Begonia semper-*	Kalanchoe
Begonia semper-	*florens*	Portulaca
florens	Caladium (tubers)	(seed or plants)
Geranium	Coleus	Sedum
Marigold	Impatiens	Sempervivum
(seed or plants)		
Nicotiana White		
Bedder		
Petunia		
Salvia		
Verbena		
Zinnia, dwarf (seed)		

Spring-flowering Bulbs. Some kinds of hardy, spring-flowering bulbs need almost no care after the first planting. Drift daffodils, scillas, crocus, snowdrops, aconites and species tulips. These can go into meadow areas where they come up and bloom while the grass is short in spring. By the time the grass grows up, or just a little later, even if it is to be moved, the bulb foliage will have matured so that clipping is not harmful. These are fine, in any rustic setting, but also near the house there is always room to bunch daffodils and other spring bulbs. Only the show-size hybrid tulips, the Darwin and breeder types, and Dutch hyacinths seem to require formal plantings, but even these can be placed in small or large groupings wherever you want spring flowers. Plant in sun or under deciduous trees, whose leaves will not be then developed enough to give too much shade. Ideally, bulbs need deeply prepared, well-drained soil, but in fact they will endure far from perfect conditions, returning spring after spring with the most welcome flowers of the season—those that come first.

Planting directions usually come with packages of spring-flowering bulbs, which are available by mail and at local garden centers from September until early November, but a good rule of thumb to remember is to plant these to a depth equal to three times the height of the individual bulb. In other words, a tulip bulb might measure 2 inches from its base to the tip, so you would plant it with about 6 inches of soil placed over the tip.

If you wish to plant spring-flowering bulbs in large containers out of doors, keep the bulbs a minimum of 6 inches away from the walls of the container. If you live in a climate where winter temperatures frequently drop to 15 degrees F. or less, push the containers up against the wall of a building and cover them, after the first hard freeze in your area, with a tarpaulin or a sheet of heavy plastic, having first mulched the surface with 5 or 6 inches of dry leaves. Remove this covering when spring weather arrives.

Perennial Flowers. The best of these stay on and on, multiplying and giving a better show each succeeding year. Some are attractive in foliage as well as in flower. Division and replanting is in order about every third or fourth year, excepting gas-plant and peony—which can be left for decades without disturbing them. Some others do well for a year or two, then decline or disappear entirely—pyrethrum and stokesia, for example—so omit these, unless you don't mind the effort of periodic replacement. Perennials sprout up from the ground in spring, freeze to the ground in fall, come back the next spring, hopefully even better than before.

Perennials may be used in countless low-upkeep ways. Plant in bays with shrubbery as a backdrop; in a bed by the terrace; in a formal garden; in a cutting garden. Use them alone, or in combination with spring-flowering bulbs, to begin the season, and with low shrubs, small trees and annuals. Most perennials need sun. A few—daylilies, hosta and monarda—can take shade, provided the soil is well prepared, humusy and moist. Astilbe and almost all ferns need shade. The magnificent hybrid lilies, which grow from bulbs available for planting in the fall or early spring, do best in perfectly drained soil that is shaded, but in a situation where the leaves receive mostly sun. One way to achieve this is to plant a low-growing annual or perennial ground cover around them; or plant the bulbs on the north side of a low wall which will keep the ground mostly shaded, but soon the emerging stems and leaves will be in full sun.

Start perennials by obtaining clumps from a local nursery or by mail—in spring (preferably) or early fall. Some are easy and inexpensive to start from seeds—Shasta daisies, pinks and cerastium, for example. Blackberry-lily (belamcanda) even blooms the first year from seeds sown indoors in a sunny window or fluorescent-light garden in February or March, then transplanted to the garden when warm weather arrives.

The aim of most of us in planting a perennial border is to have a flower bed attractive to view from the house with enough flowers for bouquets. It doesn't take many different kinds of perennials to achieve this goal. You can do it with a selection of peonies, followed by daylilies that bloom from mid-spring to late summer, and potted chrysanthemums bought in bud for fall display. Daylilies (hemerocallis) are the most notable for a long flowering season with almost no maintenance. There are hundreds of varieties, but this baker's dozen will give May-to-September bloom.

DAYLILIES FOR FIVE MONTHS OF BLOOM
(An early-to-late sequence of varieties)

Queen of Gonzales	Frances Fay	Postscript
Golden Chimes	Orange Monarch	Merry Sun
Fairy Wings	Mission Moonlight	Carved Gold
Grecian Gift	Late and Lovely	Last Dance
	George Cunningham	

Planning a perennial border that is rich in different kinds of flowers and arranging each so that the plants are complementary, with areas of the border coming pleasantly in and out of bloom, is a lot of fun, but in the same complicated way as duplicate bridge. There are astronomical variables. Sketch the size garden you want, to scale, on a sheet of paper—graph paper is fine, or draw, using 1/4 inch to equal 1 foot. Study catalog descriptions, and indicate your choices on the plan. Usually a minimum of three each should be put in a clump, but one peony or one dictamnus (gas-plant) makes a pleasant accent. You can plan a border mostly for spring flowers with a few in summer and fall; flowers from spring to frost; or a border in partial to full shade—featuring ferns, hostas, daylilies and nearly-wild flowers such as epimedium, violets and primroses.

EASY PERENNIALS FOR EDGING AND CARPETING

Alyssum Basket of Gold	Candytuft, hardy	Plumbago
Artemisia Silver Mount	Chives	Primrose
Aster, dwarf hardy	Chrysanthemum, dwarf	Santolina, Cushion
Bellflower, Carpathian	Coral Bells	Snow-in-Summer (Cerastium)
Bellflower, Serbian	Iris, dwarf bearded	Violets (white)
	Nepeta	Woolly yarrow
	Pinks (Dianthus)	

MEDIUM-HEIGHT PERENNIALS
(for midway from the front to the back of the border)

Astilbe (shade)	Chrysanthemum	Monarda
Baby's-breath	Columbine	Peony
Balloonflower	Coreopsis	Oriental poppy
Bleeding heart	Daylily	Peony
Butterfly weed	Feverfew	Shasta daisy
	Gas-plant	Veronica

TALL PERENNIALS

(for the back of the border or garden; for making
large-scale flower arrangements, especially in
containers to stand on the floor)

Achillea Gold Plate	Globe-thistle	Lily
Anchusa	Goldenglow	Lupine

Achillea	Globe-thistle	Lily
Gold Plate	Goldenglow	Lupine
Anchusa	Helenium	Lythrum
Artemisia	Hollyhock	*Phlox paniculata*
Silver King	Iris, tall bearded,	Rose-mallow
Daylily	Japanese, Spu-	Sunflower
Foxglove	ria, Siberian	Tritoma

PERENNIALS FOR A HOT, DRY SITE

Baby's-breath	Gaillardia	Sea-holly
Balloonflower	Globe-thistle	(Eryngium)
Butterfly weed	Gloriosa daisy	Sea-pink (Armeria)
Coreopsis	Golden Marguerite	*Sedum spectabile*
Daylily	Iris, bearded	Sunflower, perennial
	Pinks	Yarrow (Achillea)

Biennials for a spectacular show—next year. It's almost as risky to pigeonhole plants as it is people, but generally speaking, a biennial is a plant that spends all energy the first year growing leaves and a good root system, and the second year it blooms, sets seeds, and dies.

The list of biennial flowers reads like the roster for Great Grandmother's cottage garden: canterbury bells, foxglove, sweet William, English daisy, some forget-me-nots, hollyhock, sweet rocket, mullein, wallflower, viola, pansy, and sometimes, columbine. Great Grandmother either had more time—or, more likely—was willing to work harder, so she grew the biennials. Their two-season cycle goes like this: Sow seeds in a protected frame in July or August. Mulch well after the ground freezes in autumn. As soon as the soil can be worked in early spring, transplant to where the plants will bloom.

Biennials behave differently in different gardens and different climates. Some may even return several seasons, revealing a more perennial nature. Some, sweet rocket in particular, self-seed themselves, so that all you have to do is save selected volunteers and hoe up the others.

How To Grow Flower Gardens from Seeds

Most annual, perennial and biennial flowers for outdoors are easily started from seeds. When flowers are sown where they are to grow and bloom, the first requirement is that the soil be well prepared. Then, depending on the plan of your garden, you can sow in rows (as in a vegetable patch), in drills placed in irregularly shaped patches within a planting bed, or you can broadcast seeds in an area just as if nature might have strewn them there.

Size of seed determines to what depth you cover it with soil. Dust-size seeds—those of wax or semperflorens begonias, for example—should be started indoors under controlled conditions. But slightly larger, hardier kinds like petunia, poppy and rose-moss (portulaca) fare quite well when sown in the garden, provided the soil is well prepared to begin, and the area is kept nicely moist until the seedlings are well along. Small seeds, like the ones just mentioned, hardly need any covering at all in the garden—just pat them into the soil with the palm of your hand, or walk over the area. If you've broadcast them in a semiwild area, plant extra seeds and let nature take its course. Larger seeds—those of nasturtium, marigold and zinnia, for example—do nicely with 1/4- to 1/2-inch covering. Or cover them to a depth equal to three times their own diameter.

After seedlings have made healthy growth in the garden, you have to determine if thinning is needed. You can follow instructions given on the seed packet, or use common sense. For example, if seedlings seem to be growing weak and stretching for light, thinning is probably needed. Another rule of thumb is to think about the approximate size of a plant at maturity. Petunias that will grow about 12 inches tall will do nicely spaced 12 inches apart. Marigolds 2 feet tall might have 18- to 24-inch spacing. You can use seedlings thinned from one area to "patch" part of the row or bed that did not germinate well; simply transplant them to another part of the garden—or give them to a neighbor.

To prepare the soil for planting seeds, spread 2 inches of sphagnum peat moss or well-rotted compost over the surface; sprinkle with high-phosphorus fertilizer (5-10-5, for example), at a rate of 4 ounces per square yard. Spade, then rake smooth. Use hoe to scratch drills for sowing seeds.

Many perennials are easily grown from seed. Some will germinate in two to four weeks, although there are kinds that need to be frozen over the winter in order to sprout. Since, as a general rule, perennials need to be cool for germination, early spring is a perfect time to start them. Coldframes are good for this as they offer protection from winds and they are easily shaded and the soil therein kept moist. The most important factor for germination is constant moisture. If the seedling medium is allowed to dry out at any time, germination will be poor. Flats and seed pans are also good for starting perennials.

Vermiculite or milled sphagnum moss are both excellent to use for starting perennials, just as for house plants and annuals. Do not cover very fine seeds like those of foxglove (which is sometimes considered to be a biennial instead of a perennial), but merely sprinkle over the moist medium. Press seeds a little larger—like those of columbine—into prepared soil, vermiculite or milled sphagnum moss. Cover seeds of delphinium and lupine with about 1/8 inch; seeds the size of morning-glory 1/4 to 1/2 inch.

When the seedling plants are about an inch in height, transplant to coldframe or prepared bed in the garden where they can be watered and cared for until large enough to be set into permanent places.

Perennial seed can also be sown into open garden beds or rows in a slightly shaded location. Keep constantly moist. Thin seedlings in the rows to give enough space for vigorous, compact growth.

The list of perennials easily grown from seeds is long. Among them are such favorites as blackberry-lily, hollyhock, Shasta daisy, gaillardia, columbine, delphinium, flax, forget-me-not, lupine, lychnis, pyrethrum, sweet William, veronica, anthemis, dianthus, primrose and platycodon. More difficult, but fascinating to watch develop are iris, daylily and Christmas-rose (helleborus). Unless you go into breeding, don't bother with seeds of phlox and peonies.

How To Build Your Own Coldframe or Hotbed

A coldframe or hotbed is the ideal place for wintering-over young perennials started from seeds that season, for storing root or hardwood cuttings, and other young plants. Use 1-inch redwood boards. Set your frame on a south-facing slope, and bank into place with soil. Prepare soil and install a thermostatically-controlled heating cable. Prepared in spring, the bed gives seed planted on its surface sufficient heat for early germination and provides a headstart bed for seedlings started indoors. By fall it has become a cold frame and provides a spot to winter-over plants in the process of propagation, as well as a place to root bulbs you may be forcing for early bloom indoors—tulips, daffodils, hyacinths, for example. A propagating bed like this is also an excellent place to raise an extra-early crop of leaf lettuce and radishes in late winter.

Choice Garden Flowers To Grow from Seeds Indoors

Spend a dollar on a packet of super hybrid petunia seeds, follow instructions to the dotted line, and you can grow fifty or more fabulous plants. For even less money you can grow a garden of impatiens or everblooming wax begonias—or almost any flower you can think of. Indoors you can control light, temperature and moisture in order to successfully sprout and grow even the most delicate of tropical plants.

After you have purchased quality seeds, your next step

is selection of a growing medium. Easiest approach is to fill a pot or seed flat to 1 inch of the top with pasteurized, packaged potting soil from your local garden center. Over this place 1/2 inch vermiculite or milled sphagnum moss—sterile mediums that have the remarkable ability to hold moisture uniformly, yet allow enough air to reach roots and young stems so that disease is not likely to attack. Smooth the vermiculite or sphagnum moss and press down lightly with the bottom of a drinking glass or the palm of your hand. Broadcast seeds evenly over the surface, or sow them in shallow drills, made with a lead pencil point. If seeds are dust-fine, they are not covered. Larger seeds are covered with vermiculite or milled sphagnum moss to a depth of approximately twice to three times their own thickness.

Moisten the newly planted seeds again, to settle them, either using a hose or faucet turned to a trickle, or by adding water from a tablespoon. Place in a bright, warm spot. Be sure the surface never dries out. As soon as first leaves show, move to a place in morning sun, or in any other exposure where seedling receive at least four or five hours of sun daily. When seedlings begin to crowd, transplant to individual small pots, or to 2- by 2-inch spacing in flats. When young seedlings begin to crowd after this first transplanting, you may move them directly to the garden, or to larger pots if they are intended for growing indoors.

If you want an abundance of early-flowering annuals for your outdoor garden in summer, February or March is the ideal time for sowing most kinds. To start non-transplantables like bush sweet peas and nasturtiums, sow individual seeds in 2 1/2-inch pots of soil. Keep warm and moist. Feed every other week after growth becomes active, and keep in a sunny, airy atmosphere. If stems grow long and lanky, provide more sun, and lower temperatures if possible; also pinch out tips to cause branching. By the time you have planting-out weather, these will be near the budding stage. Heliotrope, semperflorens begonias and impatiens are better started in January, along with those of coleus for beautiful foliage.

If you have no sunny window in which to give flowers and

vegetables like tomatoes, sweet peppers and eggplant an early start, they will do just as well placed 6 inches below two 40-watt fluorescent tubes burned 16 hours out of every 24.

FLOWER SEEDS YOU CAN START INDOORS IN FEBRUARY OR MARCH

Ageratum	China-aster	Marigold	Scabiosa
Arctotis	Coleus	Nemesia	Snapdragon
Bachelor's button	Cosmos	Nicotiana	Stock
	Dahlia	Nierembergia	Sweet-alyssum
Browallia	Dianthus	Periwinkle	Sweet pea
Calendula	Dusty miller	Petunia	Torenia
Candytuft	Gazania	Phlox	Verbena
Carnation	Hibiscus	Salpiglossis	Zinnia
Celosia	Lobelia	Salvia	

Summer Flowers To Dry for Winter Bouquets

Harvesting and drying part of your summer flower crop to make winter arrangements is actually easy. Most fall into two categories: (1) kinds you tie in small, loose bunches and hang upside down to dry in an airy place, and (2) blooms you place on a layer of corn meal, borax or silica gel, and cover with the same material for a period of drying. Stems from flowers in the second category are usually removed before placing the flower in the drying agent; after the petals are chip dry, clean with a soft bristle brush, then insert wire stems and wrap with green or brown florists tape.

FLOWERS TO DRY BY HANGING, HEADS DOWN

Acacia	Tansy
Baby's-breath	Yarrow
Cockscomb	Hydrangea
Dock	Heather
Globe amaranth	Globe-thistle
Goldenrod	Pussy willow
Statice	Strawflower

FLOWERS TO DRY COVERED WITH DRYING AGENT*
(* cornmeal, borax or silica gel)

Dogwood	Feverfew
Dahlia	Clematis
Delphinium	Marigold
Larkspur	Zinnia
Carnation	Rose
Japanese anemone	Hollyhock
Queen Anne's lace	Peony
Black-eyed Susan	Dahlia

Growing for Fresh Cut Flowers

The easiest gardens of all to maintain are simple cutting plots—row on row of flowers planted like vegetables, except the crop you harvest is to feed the eye, the soul, not the stomach.

The best place for a cutting garden is a naturally well-drained plot of ground that receives at least a half day of sun. Avoid plots heavily shaded by trees and large shrubs—their shade and greedy roots will rob the cutting garden of food and light.

Whether you harvest bouquet materials from a special cutting garden, or from your annual and perennial borders, guidelines for cutting are the same. Cut flowers when they are in the peak of condition, but before they are full blown. The ideal cutting procedure is to take a pail of clean, tepid water right into the garden with you. Use sharp shears to cut each stem, immediately plunge the base in water, and re-cut a half inch of stem under water. This assures that no air bubbles prevent the flow of water into the stems.

If stems have a milky or glutinous sap that exudes from them, further conditioning will be needed. This applies to such favorite flowers as poppies (glutinous sap) and poinsettias (milky sap). You can condition them by charring the lower half inch of the stem over a flame, or you can dip about a half inch of the stem base in boiling water. These measures simply seal the life of the flower into the stem so that you can enjoy it for the maximum time in a bouquet.

Woody stems—lilacs and chrysanthemums, for example—need to be crushed; the lower inch is sufficient, and you can use a hammer or wooden mallet. After crushing, plunge immediately into water of room temperature or slightly warmer. The amazing thing is that you can re-cut and crush woody-stemmed flowers every other day or two to further prolong life. This technique is especially effective with lilacs.

Do copper pennies or aspirin really make cut flowers last longer? Unfortunately, no—keep your pennies and aspirin for conventional uses. But a teaspoon of sugar to a pint of water may prolong the life of cut flowers, just as the commercially prepared cut-flower preservatives may prove beneficial.

The best time to cut flowers is in the early evening; next best is early in the morning. By noon and early afternoon, many flowers may be in a slightly wilted condition, and some kinds never recover after being cut, regardless of the best conditioning techniques.

Flowers To Attract Butterflies

Imagine an idyllic garden scene. Fragrant flowers. Lofty shade trees. The splash of water. Goldfish streaking a lily pool. Birds singing. Now, all you need for perfection are butterflies dancing about the blossoms.

However ethereal and elusive butterflies may seem, they can in fact be invited or attracted to your garden. It's all a matter of selecting flowers rich in nectar they can extract easily. The list of flowers is surprisingly long, and contains mostly common plants. For example: purple and crimson aubrieta, yellow alyssum, creeping phlox, primroses, bluebells, white arabis, perennial candytuft, wallflowers and sweet rocket for spring.

Summer flowers to feed the butterflies include mignonette, scabiosa, thyme, lavender, hyssop, rosemary, catnip, phlox, gaillardia, lantana, and of course the butterfly bush (buddleia). Toward autumn, butterflies will feast on showy stonecrop (*Sedum spectabile*), Michaelmas daisies and goldenrod.

Chapter 7
VEGETABLES, HERBS AND BERRIES

No vegetable, herb, berry or fruit sold can compare in flavor with home-grown produce. For one thing, only home-grown edibles can be allowed to ripen on the plant until they have reached the perfect moment for picking and eating. For another, only if the tomatoes, corn or beans are growing in your garden can you pick them just moments before they are to be cooked and served, and that's how fresh produce should be to capture peak flavor and nutrition. Another reason home garden crops are so much better is that the home gardener can plant those superior but delicate varieties too tender for commercial picking, handling and long-term storage. And beyond these practical benefits, there is the sheer joy of harvesting food you have chosen, planted and watched grow in your own garden.

Where To Plant Your Food Crops

All food plants require well-drained soil and a lot of sunlight. Any spot in your landscape will do for vegetables, herbs, fruit plants and nut trees as long as these two needs are met. A southern slope that offers protection from north winds is an excellent site, and if your soil happens to be a sandy loam that warms quickly in spring, the situation is just about ideal. Avoid steep slopes where soil will erode and really low spots where late and early frosts settle. Keep food plants away from airless corners where pests and diseases prosper, and keep vegetable gardens away from big trees that will compete for soil moisture and nutrients. If you can, locate the vegetables near your water supply and tool-shed. If you live in a wooded area, try to set food plants as close to the house as possible to discourage furry pests from raiding.

Unless you are in the business of growing food, another consideration in your choice of site for food plants is how they will look from the living areas of the house and grounds. Many of the food plants are quite beautiful and can be fitted into the landscape with pleasure.

Fruit trees cover themselves with beautiful white and pink blossoms in spring and can be used instead of their more glamorous cousins, the flowering fruit trees, which are bred for ornament rather than for fruit. Many nut trees are stately specimens worth growing for shade alone. Low-growing nut trees and the dwarf fruits can be set in pairs to border a garden path, and blueberries make a handsome hedge that glows with scarlet leaves in fall. Grape vines make glorious arbors and can be trained high enough to shade a picture window or a terrace.

Vegetable crops that go into the ground and come out a few weeks later belong out of sight, as do such things as pole beans and cornstalks. But some vegetables have value as ornamentals and can be grown in flower borders. Rhubarb, a perennial with great ripple-edged leaves and creamy flower stalks, can be used as a low deciduous hedge or in planters. Asparagus, another perennial, sends up dreamy feathery fronds after the crop has gone, and looks lovely planted in among flowers. Tomatoes staked upright and held secure by plant twist-ties can make handsome ornamentals. Cherry tomatoes and green peppers are charming in the flower border, too. In fact, these food plants, with herbs and salad greens and combined shaggy cactus zinnias, tall and small marigolds, and bedding petunias, make attractive food and flower gardens that can be sited anywhere.

Once you have decided how big or small your garden can be, rule a sketch of it and make a list of the vegetables most wanted. Allowing 2 to 3 feet per row, write in the plantings selected, along with the date they should be planted, and when the crops should be ready. Catalogs usually list days to maturity beside each vegetable seed packet offered. Note that the types called "early" are generally faster to mature, while "midseason" and "late" varieties are meant to be planted in early spring and won't be ready until summer or fall. When "early" varieties have finished producing crops, a second and sometimes a third sowing of quick-harvest vegetables such as lettuce, radishes, snap bush beans, can sometimes be planted in these spaces. This is called "succession cropping." Extra crops can be fitted in by planting vining types, such as squash and cucumbers, at the foot of tall crops, such as corn. This is called "companion planting."

Vegetable Seeds Are Easy To Plant

Shake a small amount of seed into one hand. Sow by pinching some seed between thumb and forefinger of the other hand, then easing the seed into the soil which you have previously prepared.

You can get a headstart on your garden by setting it to grow on a sunny window sill indoors four to six weeks before weather warms sufficiently for setting in the outdoor garden. Start seeds indoors in small flats, pots of peat, clay or plastic, or pans filled with horticultural vermiculite, a sterile starting medium you can buy at nurseries and garden centers.

Sprinkle seed on the soil; cover each kind to a depth suited to its own size—about three times its thickness. Moisten the planting from the bottom and set in a light area. When seedlings appear, place in a sunny window. As seedling leaves touch one another, thin or transplant to individual pots filled with equal parts garden soil, peat moss and sand. Plants growing in peat pots can be set into the garden without unpotting.

Before transplanting to the garden, harden plants off by setting them in a cool, protected area such as under a low shrub or on an unheated porch.

If you are planting directly into the outdoor garden, you'll find most vegetables do well planted in shallow furrows in areas where moisture is plentiful; on ridges between furrows in areas where furrows make irrigation easier.

Pole beans, cucumbers, corn, melons and squash are often planted in hills, eight to ten seeds in a 10- to 16-inch circle. Thin each hill to the sturdiest three or four plants.

Interplant rapid-growing varieties such as beets or radishes between slower-growing vegetables, such as cabbage or corn. Rapid growers will push above soil line and be ready for harvesting before slower types start shading them.

Rotate crops for best garden yield and as protection against insects. Different types of vegetables use different soil elements, attract different insects. Root crops, heavy in their use of potash and phosphorus, should be followed by leaf crops or legumes such as peas or beans, which need less of these elements.

For top production and early crops, supply your vegetable garden with good garden loam. Good garden loam has a structure composed of roughly one third sand, one third clay or soil, one third humus. Food plants flourish in soils with a pH of between 6.0 and 6.8. Working with an inexpensive soil testing kit, you can determine how much of what materials your soil requires to attain the correct pH (*see also* Chapter 1).

Vegetable	Plant Outdoors	Depth in Inches	Row Spacing	Space Apart in Rows
Asparagus	Mar.-Apr.	1	12 in.	1 ft.
Beans, bush	Apr.-May	2	2-3 ft.	4-5 in.
Beans, bush lima	Apr.-May	2	18-24 in.	10-12 in.
Beans, pole	Apr.-May	2	4 ft.	3 ft.
Beets	May	1	15 in.	4 in.
Broccoli	Mar.	1/2	30 in.	2 ft.
Cabbage, Chinese	Mar.	1/2	18-24 in.	8-12 in.
Cabbage, early	Mar.-Apr.	1/2	3 ft.	18-36 in.
Cabbage, late	May	1	3 ft.	2-3 ft.
Carrots	Mar.-Apr.	3/4	14 in.	2-4 in.
Cauliflower	Apr.	1/2	3 ft.	2 ft.
Celery	June	1/4	4-5 ft.	6 in.
Cucumbers	May	1	6 ft.	3 ft.
Eggplant	May	1/2	3 ft.	30 in.
Lettuce	Mar.-Apr.	1/2	14 in.	6 in.
Muskmelons	May	1	6 ft.	3 ft.
Onions	Mar.-Apr.	3/4	14 in.	4 in.
Onion sets	Mar.-Apr.	2	1 ft.	2-3 in.
Parsnips	Mar.-Apr.	1/2	15 in.	4-5 in.
Peas, smooth	Mar.-Apr.	2	2 ft.	3 in.
Peas, wrinkled	May	2	2 ft.	3 in.
Peppers	May	1/2	3 ft.	2 ft.
Popcorn	May	1-1/2	3 ft.	10 in.
Pumpkin	May	1-1/2	12 ft.	1-2 ft.
Radish	Mar.-Apr.	1	14 in.	2-3 in.
Salsify	Mar.-Apr.	1	14 in.	2 in.
Spinach	Mar.	3/4-1	14 in.	3-4 in.
Squash	May	1-1/2	12 ft.	12 ft.
Sweet corn	May	2	3 ft.	12 in.
Tomato plants	May	4-6	3 ft.	3 ft.
Turnips	Mar.	1/2	15 in.	5-8 in.
Watermelons	May	1-1/2	18 ft.	10 ft.

Vegetables are heavy feeders. For row crops, apply fertilizer in bands 2 to 4 inches from the plants and dig the bands into the soil 3 to 4 inches deep. Follow labels for proper amount of applications. Cover the fertilizer with soil. Water thoroughly after application. Wash off fertilizer dusted on the foliage. Several light applications during the season are more effective than one or two shots of fertilizer in heavier doses.

Watering, Weeding and Mulching for a Super Crop

Overhead sprinkling with a vegetable and home garden sprinkler is one excellent way to keep your edibles growing steadily and succulent, even in dry weather. A bubbler-soaker attachment is recommended also for deep, effective watering.

Mulching with peat moss, leaf mold, rotted manure or black polyethylene film will cut down on weed growth and make soil more moisture retentive. Apply 2-inch blankets of organic mulches when the soil is warm and plants have pushed a few inches above the soil. Apply black polyethylene (black plastic) film in runners, between planted rows, making slits in film near plants so moisture can seep through.

If weeds appear before mulch is applied, rake loose, or hoe to uproot. Remember that weeds dug when really tiny are easy to handle, but by the time they have grown into plants inches tall, they can be tougher than molars to pull or cut loose.

Herbs and Salad Gardens

There's great enthusiasm today for home-grown vegetables, but the idea of undertaking a whole kitchen garden can seem like a big project to the beginner. If your nerve is not strong enough for the total kitchen garden approach, or if your space is limited, back into the growing of vegetables via salad makings and herbs. The garden doesn't have to be big to provide greens and tomatoes and cucumbers and onions and all the herbs you can use fresh during the growing season, or dried during the winter. An herb garden can be as little as a window box, set outdoors or on a sunny window sill indoors.

Both salad makings and herbs will flourish in a small plot by the kitchen door or on small, stepped terraces by the patio. Try a few this season: they're all so easy to grow you'll want to add a few varieties, at least, next year—and one day may graduate to the handsome, traditional herb-scented spaces of a Victorian knot garden.

Herbs we commonly use for cooking have nearly all come from the arid, sunny coasts of the Mediterranean Sea, and are most successful in conditions that reproduce their well-drained native soil and light-drenched climate. This doesn't mean you can let them thirst to death, but it does mean that soils and containers for the growing of herbs should have a good proportion of sand and small pebbles to ensure that the plants' roots never sit in puddles of muddy water.

Almost any container is suited to a small collection of herbs. Try a group of *fines herbes*, parsley, thyme, basil, chives for instance, in a hanging basket or in a strawberry-jar set on a sunny corner of the terrace.

Fill a window box with your favorites and bring some indoors at the end of the season. Some of the woody stemmed herbs such as rosemary can be kept from year to year and trained to ornamental tree form. If you live high in a city skyscraper, grow the shrubby, larger herb perennials, such as lemon-verbena and lavender, in tubs.

To ensure good drainage for these pot-grown plants, make holes in the bottoms of the containers, and set them on trays containing pebbles which can be kept filled with water. The pebbles allow the plants to draw some water without actually sitting in it.

You can grow lettuces and onions and tomatoes and all the salad makings you could want, even on a rooftop, if the planting soil is right and your containers take into account the needs of the plants you want to grow.

In deep, well-drained wooden boxes, a variety of garden produce will flourish, including leaf lettuce, the heading lettuces such as Bibb and Boston, cucumber vines, espaliered cherry tomatoes and even the big, sweet Bermuda onions, which are usually grown from started seedlings or sets purchased from catalogs or at your local garden center in the spring. You can also line peck, half-bushel and bushel baskets with plastic and fill them with planting soil in order to grow a container garden of edibles at the lowest possible cost.

Growing Herbs as House Plants

The rules for growing herbs indoors are simple and similar to those for growing herbs in containers outdoors. The most important is that you provide well-drained pebbly soil and set the pots or other containers in trays filled with an inch or two of moist sand or pebbles. Group the plants together to create a little climate which is moist—the plants really flourish. At least once a week, wash off the foliage of potted herbs in water at room temperature, and the plants will respond as happily as outdoor plants do when freshed by a summer shower. Turn the pots and baskets in the window about once a week to keep them from growing lopsided toward the light. Pinch out growing tips often to encourage bushiness. Provide as much fresh air as is practical.

Chives, dill, chervil, basil, sweet bay, borage, catnip, coriander, the scented geraniums, lavender, lemon balm, sweet marjoram, the mints, if contained in deep large pots, rosemary, sage, winter savory and thyme—all will succeed indoors. The herbs also grow as well in fluorescent light as they do in sunny indoor spots, so try this method if yours is a dwelling without any bright windows.

How To Harvest Your Herbs

You can pick leaves or branch tips of herbs any time after the plant is obviously flourishing. The best time for harvesting is when flower buds are beginning to open—for most but not all herbs. Pick the crops in the morning after the dew is dry, but before the sun has begun to volatilize the essential oils that contain the herb's flavor. Cut perennials down by one third when harvesting the plant for winter storage and pull annuals up by their roots, or cut back to one third their size if you want to reserve some fresh growing leaves until frost time.

Rinse away grit with a sink spray, dry at once gently with paper toweling, spread between screens in a single layer to dry, and leave in a dark, airy room until crackly crisp. Or dry hung by the stems in small bunches in a well-ventilated attic for ten days or more. Dried in a brown paper bag, these bunches will be dust-free until ready to strip from the branches and be stored in airtight containers.

To harvest herb seeds, watch for the moment in late summer, when seedheads show signs of being ready to loosen their hold on the seeds. Cut heads without shaking into a linen-lined basket and dry in an airy spot. When heads are very dry, thresh out seed by rubbing seedheads between your palms outdoors where the breeze will blow away the chaff. Spread the seeds to dry for ten days or so on cheesecloth set on a screen, then store in airtight containers for winter.

Fruits for Your Own Orchard

The orchard fruits grow on trees and include apples, pears, peaches, plums, cherries and the citrus fruits. With little more care and attention than is required by a shrub, they yield delicious crops year after year. With careful selection of varieties that produce at different periods, you can have fresh fruit most of the year. Finding varieties that will flourish in your area and provide a succession of fruits isn't difficult. Notify your local Agricultural Extension Service (check under government, U.S., listings in the Yellow Pages) of the types of fruit you want to grow and ask which varieties are most suited to your location. By careful selection of variety and with good storage, it is possible to have apples from July through winter, pears from late July to March, plums, peaches and nectarines from July until October and cherries from June through mid-August. The fast-bearing, easy-to-handle dwarf and semidwarf varieties yield about 1 to 3 bushels per tree for the dwarfs and 5 to 10 bushels for the semidwarfs.

Cross-pollination is an important factor in the yield from orchard fruits. Most apples and pears require cross-pollination to set fruit. So do most plums. Most peaches and nectarines are self-pollinators, but not all. Sour cherries, the cherries so good in pies, are self-pollinators, but most varieties of sweet cherries are not. Species that require cross-pollination are species that will not produce fruit unless pollen from a suitable other variety is carried by insects or the elements to the flowers of the species requiring pollination. Garden centers and catalogs can tell you whether the species and varieties of orchard tree you wish to grow require a pollinator, and can suggest suitable pollinators.

Orchard fruits are planted in the same way as other trees and flourish in the garden loam in which vegetables succeed best and which is described earlier in this chapter. Site should be well-drained, and in cooler sections of the country some protection from winter winds is desirable.

However anxious you may be to preserve ecological balance, in many sections it is necessary to institute a yearly spraying program in order to guarantee good fruit crops. The accompanying table includes a suggested spray program for the most popular orchard fruits and some of the bramble fruits.

Almost everyone can have a strawberry patch. These hardy and exquisite fruits are produced by low-growing perennial plants that produce one crop a year, early, mid-season or late, or in the ever-bearer varieties, one large crop in late spring, a scattering of berries throughout summer and a late summer crop. Two dozen plants of two or three varieties keep a family in berries for most of the season. Most gardeners keep runners cut away and change the berry patch every four to five years in order to keep berries at top quality. If plantlets or runners of the berry plants are allowed to root all season long, the patch becomes a matted row and in time the berries do become smaller. A popular system for the berry patch is to allow berries to set no fruit the first season (keep flowers picked before they go to seed and become berries), and to keep all runners cut. Second season, harvest crops, and keep runners cut. Third season, harvest as before, let each plant set two runners, which become young plants at season's end. Fourth season, cut away and plant in a new patch last season's young plantlets, harvest old plants as before. Fifth season, harvest crop from new patch, dig up and discard old patch.

FRUIT YIELD CHART AND SPRAY SCHEDULE

Fruit	Yield	Spray Dates
Dwarf apple	1-2 bushels	FIRST: When buds show pink, but before blossoms open.
Semi-dwarf apple	2-3 bushels	SECOND: As soon as petals have fallen.
Dwarf pear	1-2 bushels	THIRD: Ten days later.
Semi-dwarf pear	1-3 bushels	FOURTH: Two weeks later. FIFTH: Two weeks later, but omit for early varieties. SIXTH: Two weeks later.
Dwarf peach	1-2 bushels	FIRST: While plant is still dormant in very early spring.
Semi-dwarf peach	2-3 bushels	SECOND: As soon as petals have fallen.
Nectarine	3-4 bushels	THIRD: Ten days later. FOURTH: One week later. FIFTH: Two weeks later. SIXTH: Six weeks later.
Semi-dwarf plum	1-2 bushels	FIRST: As soon as petals fall.
Standard Plum	2-4 bushels	SECOND: Ten days later.
Standard sour cherry	1-2 bushels	THIRD: One week later.
Semi-dwarf sweet cherry	1-2 bushels	FOURTH: Two weeks later, but omit for early varieties of sweet cherry.
Raspberry	1-1/2 qts.	No spray needed.
Blackberry	1-1/4 qts.	No spray needed.
Blueberry	4 qts.	No spray needed.
Grapes	15-30 pounds	FIRST: When new growth is 1/2-2 in. SECOND: When shoots 4-8 in. THIRD: One week after bloom. FOURTH: Three weeks later. FIFTH: Four weeks before harvest.

Blueberries are easy on the gardener, providing the soil is really acid, with a pH between 4.4 and 5.1. If your soil tends to be alkaline, you can grow them by adding two parts acid peat moss to one part garden loam and establishing the plants in barrels or boxed trenches, but it's a lot of work. Blueberries are among the plants requiring cross-pollination, but this is easy to achieve since any two varieties will cross-pollinate each other. Don't let new plants set fruit for the first two years. They'll go on producing for a dozen years or more, so you can afford to wait. The only pruning needed is the removal of excessive small growth and dead branches or twigs in the spring of each year. The blueberry crop ripens over a six-week period and will need some protection from the birds. Netting sold in hardware stores is effective. Or you can plant nearby flowering shrubs whose ornamental berries will attract your feathered friends away from the blueberry bushes.

Grapes will grow on poor soils where not too many other fruit plants will flourish. They are now hardy and the rather sour Concords, excellent for jellies, that were the only grapes possible for the northern home garden, are being replaced by delicious, sweet table grapes of four or five varieties. Grapes should be set in a very sunny, well-drained location in soil well supplied with humus. Set the plants 8 to 10 feet apart and plant in early spring while the ground is still cool and moist. Plant as you would a small tree, then cut the vine back to above the two lowest buds. Train the branches that develop from these two buds as shown in the accompanying sketch, and for maximum production, prune as shown. Grapes will produce the second or third year after planting and will go on producing for decades. A few varieties require cross-pollination, but most do not. Mulch to keep the ground weed-free and to preserve moisture. Water the plants when they begin to set fruit. In early spring, fertilize with a handful of compost or with the fertilizer recommended by your garden center. It is necessary in many sections to spray grapes as you do orchard fruits. For a spray schedule, see the table on page 108.

You Can Grow Nuts for Shade and Bounty

Though some of the best nuts can be grown in home orchards only in milder regions of the country, there are now many excellent new varieties that will succeed in cooler climates, among them butternuts, filberts and some new paper-shell pecans, black walnuts and hickory. Select varieties offered as named or grafted trees since these bear in two to three years instead of the five to ten years required by many of the self-rooted types. Cross-pollination seems to produce higher yields in most nut species, so plant two varieties of whatever type you choose.

Allow the nuts to fully mature on the tree and to fall to the ground of themselves. Gather the nuts as soon as possible after they have fallen. This is easier if old sheets have been spread under the branches. Husk the nuts and spread them in their shells on screens in thin layers. Allow them to dry for several days before storing.

The butternut is just about the hardiest of the northern climate species. It belongs to the walnut family and is a native tree from New Brunswick to Arkansas. The trees reach to about 75 feet at maturity and flourish in rich soils and near stream banks. Although butternut shells can be very hard to crack, some of the new varieties offered by garden catalogs have thinner shells. A beautiful, long-lived tree, the butternut is self-pollinating.

The chestnuts that grew wild in America in the days of the pioneers have been wiped out by a blight that has attacked the trees since the turn of the century. However, in the home garden they can be successfully replaced by the Chinese chestnuts. Smaller and less hardy than the native species, Chinese chestnuts succeed where peach trees thrive. They reach to about 40 feet at maturity, yield nuts that are a little smaller than the American and European species and must be planted in two varieties as they require cross-pollination. Named varieties have been bred which are even more blight-resistant than the original Chinese chestnut; be sure you plant two different named varieties.

The walnuts are probably the most generally popular of all the nuts and among the most beautiful of nut trees. The English walnut originally came from Persia and is the walnut whose crop is sold commercially in supermarkets. It is a close relative of the winter-hardy black walnut (which pioneers named the "white walnut"). Walnuts reach to a height of 100 feet at maturity and grow well in sections where peaches succeed. Several new varieties are hardier than the peach tree, among them the much advertised Carpathian walnut from Poland, a smaller tree that grows to about 50 feet tall. Walnuts succeed in rich, well-drained soils, but should not be fertilized too heavily in cooler regions.

The heart nut, or Japanese walnut, is considered to have better shelling qualities than the Carpathian variety and produces an excellent nut meat. Often called the Japanese walnut, it isn't quite as hardy as the Carpathian. Black walnuts are hardier than English walnuts, but are in danger in areas where winters can go below 20 below zero. Some of the cultivated varieties are improved and are worth trying if wild black walnuts grow in your climate. Walnuts must be cross-pollinated, so plant two varieties. When the nuts fall, gather and husk at once, then wash the shells, air dry them, and layer on screens to dry further in a dark, airy room.

The filberts and the hazelnuts belong to the same genus, and distinctions between the two are so minor as to cause a lot of confusion. The true filbert of southeastern Europe has oblong nuts in long husks. The hazelnuts have roundish nuts in short husks. Popularly, the two names are synonymous. Improved hybrid forms now offered by catalogs and at garden centers generally succeed where peaches are hardy, and are very successful in the Northwest. They are small, pretty trees that fit well into suburban landscapes and will succeed as far south as southern Pennsylvania. Plant them in a rich, well-drained soil and give protection from north winds. Prune them as you do peaches, but not too severely. Two or more filbert trees should be planted to ensure a good yield, but they needn't be of different varieties.

House Plants When You Go On Vacation: Unless you have a reliable plantsitter to water your plants while you are away from home for a week or more, it will be necessary to make some provision for satisfying their needs in your absence. One solution is a Melnor vacation and hospital plant care kit that has been introduced recently. This is available in three sizes: large, for big upright plants and hanging types; small to medium for things like African violets, begonias and ferns; and mixed, to accomodate the varied sizes of plants that make up most collections.

Each kit consists essentially of specially treated plastic bags, twist-ties and plant support structures. Before placing a plant in the bag, go over it carefully to be sure it is totally free of insects; also remove any yellowing or dead leaves and spent flowers; then check the soil and add water if necessary so that when the plant goes in the bag its soil is uniformly moist.

You can even place several plants in one large bag. Once your plants are all bagged, with the supports in place where needed, and the opening is secured with a twist-tie, place them where they receive as much bright light as possible, but little or no direct sun. Plants prepared in this fashion may be left for several days or up to four weeks with no worry about their drying up and dying while you are away.

Chapter 8
BRINGING IN THE OUTDOORS

No matter how many gardens you have outdoors, there is nothing quite so rewarding as having thriving plants in the rooms where you live. Watching and helping them grow is in fact a miraculous kind of modern-day therapy that has already proven beneficial for people of all ages and states in life.

One amazing thing about house plants is that if you care enough to keep the soil nicely moist at all times—never bone dry or dripping wet for days on end—most will adapt, given a pleasantly bright or sunny place. This is why the colorful croton which grows outdoors in Florida in full sun can be found thriving in a north-facing New York City apartment. Or a Boston fern, generally thought to be a shade plant needing coolness, may be found in someone's south-facing picture window in full sun with heat seeming to pour on it from a radiator. But potted plants cannot survive a dark room in the daytime or really careless watering practices.

Before you invest in plants, study the amount of light that comes through your doors and windows. Photosynthesis, the process by which plants grow, is triggered by light. Plants vary in the amount they need, but most perform satisfactorily in a wide range of intensities. Flowering plants and foliages discussed in this chapter are keyed to the four basic light categories for indoor gardening:

(1) **Sunny** suggests a window facing south;

(2) **Semi-sunny** suggests a window facing west;

(3) **Semi-shady** suggests a window facing east;

(4) **Shady** suggests a window facing north.

If house plants have the proper amount of water and heat for good growth, but do not have enough light, they tend to grow long and spindly. Often, planters are used as decorating accessories in locations that are not lighted well enough for you to find a number in your telephone directory, much less grow healthy plants. However, foliage plants can be acclimated to low-light intensities.

To grow foliage plants where they get little or no bright daylight:

(1) Water the plants only often enough to prevent wilting.

(2) Reduce the amount of fertilizer that you apply to the plants.

(3) Keep the air temperature as cool as you can tolerate.

(4) Provide supplementary lighting with fluorescent tubes or incandescent floodlights.

FOLIAGE PLANTS MOST LIKELY TO SUCCEED IN DIM LIGHT

Aglaonema (Chinese evergreen)
Asparagus-fern
Aspidistra (cast-iron plant)
Chamaedorea (palm)
Chlorophytum (spider-plant)
Cissus (grape-ivy)
Cyperus (umbrella plant)
Dieffenbachia (dumbcane)
Dracaena (corn plant)
Ficus (fig or rubber plant)
Hedera helix (English ivy)
Monstera (Swiss cheese plant)

Nephrolepis (Boston fern)
Ophiopogon (lily-turf)
Philodendron
Pittosporum
Podocarpus
Polystichum (fern)
Sansevieria (snake plant)
Schefflera
Scindapsus (pothos)
Spathiphyllum (peace-lily)
Syngonium (nephthytis)

Gardening with Artificial Light

If our natural light is not bright enough to grow plants, or if you want to grow plants in a part of the room where natural light is weak, install artificial lighting. A fluorescent set-up is perhaps easiest, since units designed specifically for growing plants are available for instant turn-on. Most of these contain either two 20-watt tubes in a reflector that measures 24 inches long and about 12 inches wide, or two 40-watt tubes in a reflector 48 inches long by 12 inches wide. The smaller unit will light a table or shelf growing area up to 24 inches long by 18 inches wide. The larger unit will give you a growing area measuring two by four feet—in other words, eight square feet in which to cultivate flowering or foliage house plants, or to start seeds and cuttings to bring to maturity in your outdoor garden. Burn the lights 14 to 16 hours out of every 24. Although special growth fluorescents are on the market, a combination of one ordinary Cool White with one Warm White will produce excellent leaf and flower growth.

Incandescent floodlights for growing plants are generally available in wattages varying from 75 to 150. Purchase reflector floods and screw them into a ceramic or porcelain socket.

Smaller sizes can be placed within 18 to 24 inches of the leaves, larger sizes 24 to 36 inches away, so as not to burn tender leaves or flowerbuds. Direct the light from above or to the side of the plant, not from below. If the plants receive weak daylight, burn the floods 6 to 8 hours daily; if the sole source of light, burn the floods 14 to 16 hours out of every 24. Since the heat given off by incandescents tends to dry out the air, it will help your plants thrive if you mist the leaves frequently and place the pots in pebble humidity trays—or use a cool-vapor humidifier in the same room throughout the winter heating season.

Most house plants will prosper in the same kind of temperatures that people find comfortable. Specifically, a range of 60 to 80 degrees F. During the winter heating season, it is preferable not to have temperatures much higher than 75 degrees F. If you want to grow a plant known to need cooler temperatures, look around your rooms and windows; often one room can be kept cooler, either by lowering the thermostat, keeping a window lowered slightly from the top (so that cold air does not blow directly on the plant—or plants), or by shutting off the radiator or other heating unit within the room—which might be a guest bedroom which you use only occasionally.

Humidity—the amount of moisture contained by the air surrounding your plants—goes hand in hand with proper temperatures. The higher the humidity, the lower the temperatures can be for human comfort. In other words, if you have a Sahara atmosphere with less than 10 percent relative humidity, temperatures may have to range between 70 and 80 degrees in order for you to be comfortable. However, if the humidity is 30 percent or more, temperatures of 68 to 72 degrees F. will make you feel comfortable—and the total atmosphere will be much more healthful for plants as well as people, fine wood furnishings—and the piano.

The best way to evaluate the amount of humidity in your home is to invest in an inexpensive hygrometer—an instrument that indicates on an easily read dial the percentages of relative humidity in the air. Most plants do best with 30 percent or more. You can increase humidity simply by grouping a large number of plants together.

Place the pots of your plants in pebble humidity trays—shallow, waterproof trays in which you place a layer of pebbles, and then keep filled with water to a level that does not quite reach the bottoms of the pots, otherwise the roots and soil will soak up more water than they need.

Frequent misting of house plant leaves is often thought to increase humidity. It does—for a few minutes, or even up to an hour—but if you want constant humidity, use pebble trays. And if you decide your plants need even more humidity, invest in a cool-vapor humidifier. Room-size units are sold by most pharmacies and drugstores for the treatment of respiratory illnesses. Most of these units sell for under $30 and hold up to 2 gallons of water; you will have to refill such a unit twice every 24 hours. Larger units will humidify two or three rooms; these hold six to 17 gallons of water and will need to be filled every two or three days. Misting house plant leaves is beneficial, however, even though it doesn't do much to keep up the level of humidity. Misting helps keep the leaves clean, shiny and healthy—and it is a pleasant activity for you.

How much and how often to water house plants seems to be a big puzzler for a lot of people. It needn't be. Virtually all potted plants do well in soil that is nicely moist at all times. Right after you apply water—which should be of room temperature—the soil will be wet, but within a few hours the excess should evaporate (or you should pour off any water remaining in the pot saucer) and the surface soil will then feel nicely moist to your fingers. When the surface soil begins to feel dry, water the plant well. Do not wait for the leaves to wilt. If you do, new leaves may wither and die; old leaves will turn yellow and die prematurely; and any flowerbuds that may have been forming will literally have been nipped in the bud.

There are two conditions to avoid in watering your plants—the extremes of wet and dry. Virtually no plant can tolerate standing day after day, week after week in a saucer of water. And no plant, not even a cactus from the desert, can survive having a pot of soil that is completely dry. When experts advise letting the soil "dry out" between waterings, they don't mean bone dry; they mean the soil should dry out slightly.

House plants will grow in a variety of soil mixtures. Although you can, theoretically, dig soil from your garden and use it for potting, results are generally better if you start with a packaged potting soil. You will find these at your nursery, garden center or plant shop pre-packaged and labeled for specific types of plants. For example, all-purpose packaged potting soil, foliage-plant soil, flowering-plant or African violet soil, cactus/succulent and terrarium.

In practice, most indoor gardeners find that packaged all-purpose potting soils give better results if two or three parts of the all-purpose soil is mixed with one part each of sphagnum peat moss and vermiculite, two organic ingredients you will also find in packages of convenient size wherever plants are sold. And, if you want to grow a cactus or other succulent, but have only all-purpose or flowering-plant potting soil on hand, simply mix two parts of this with one part of sand or perlite (an organic, lightweight substitute for sand). If you are careful not to over- or underwater, you can grow almost any plant in any of these potting mixtures. If you want to keep your fingernails clean while potting, wear handy disposable gloves.

During spring and summer, potted plants usually benefit from being fed with a prepared house-plant fertilizer, following directions on the container. Concentrates are available in liquid or granular forms; dilute in water of room temperature, following container directions, and apply only to soil that is already nicely moist, never when it is bone dry. There are also liquid house-plant fertilizers on the market formulated to apply directly to the soil, and there are pelletized, time-release capsules you apply to the surface of the soil three or four times a year. If the plant you want to feed is being cultivated primarily for foliage, feed with a foliage-plant fertilizer (which will have a high nitrogen content). If you are growing a flowering plant such as a geranium, feed it with a blossom-booster type fertilizer, often labeled specifically for African violets.

Plants will grow well in almost any kind of container that has a drainage hole in the bottom. If you are very careful about watering, you can even grow plants in jardinieres or cachepots that have no provision for drainage. It is important to realize that unglazed clay pots evaporate moisture through the walls and require watering more frequently than plastic or glazed ceramic pots, the walls of which are sealed and do not allow moisture to escape.

After a period of growing, watering and fertilizing, an unglazed pot will often develop a salty, grayish-white encrustation on the edges and outside surface. This is a buildup of mineral salts from the water and fertilizer. Remove by scrubbing with a soap pad or stiff brush, then rinse in clean water.

When you want to pot up a seedling or rooted cutting, or transplant a plant from a smaller to a larger pot, what size pot to use can be confusing. A good rule of thumb in this dilemma is to select a pot whose diameter (the distance across the top) equals one-half to one-third the height of a plant if it is upright growing, or its width if it grows primarily in a horizontal plane. In other words, you would put an 18-inch palm in a 6- to 9-inch pot; an African violet 9 inches across would look right and grow well in a 3- to 5-inch pot.

Plants need to be repotted when roots fill the present container. You can tell by removing the pot, although this isn't necessary if you see roots creeping out of the drainage hole at the bottom, in which case you'll know it is time to repot.

Bugs likely to attack your house plants at one time or another include cottony white mealybugs, white flies, red spider-mites, aphids and brown scale. Pyrethrum sprays will control aphids; use malathion for mealybugs, white flies and brown scale; use a miticide such as Dimite or Kelthane on red spider-mites. The trend today is to wash off as many of the insects as possible in tepid water to which a little mild soap has been added (then rinse in clear water), especially a product like Melnor's new plant soap. If this kind of treatment fails, then you can resort to spraying or dipping the plant in a pesticide.

Red spider-mites in particular deserve special attention. They are tiny and not easily detected without a magnifying glass, until the plant leaves show a mottled yellow appearance and tiny webs may be detected between the leaves and the stems. Red spider-mites thrive in an atmosphere that is too hot, dry and stale. It does little good to spray mite-infested plants unless you improve the environment at the same time.

If you develop the habit of regularly grooming your house plants by showering the leaves in tepid water, trimming off dead ones or spent flowers, and generally staying in close communication with them (this doesn't mean you have to talk), you are much less likely to suddenly discover that they are covered with bugs. Time spent in grooming your plants can be highly therapeutic—both for you and them.

You can be a more confident, and therefore more successful, indoor gardener, if you take advantage of some of the metering devices available today. For example, soil moisture meters (often in combination with a light meter), have probes which you insert deep into the pot, where the root action is, to determine by a readout on the meter whether the soil down there is wet, moist, on the dry side, or dry. Light meters take away the guesswork as to whether the light is bright or dim in terms of plant needs. Of course, buying the meter won't make your plants grow better unless you use it and follow the care its readout suggests.

Foliage Plants for Decorating Your Home

Acorus is a white-and-green grass to grow indoors. *A. gramineus* forms a grassy spray about 10 inches tall. Its variety *pusillus* grows in fans of leaves only 3 inches tall. Provide as much coolness as possible in the winter—a range of 60-70 degrees F. is acceptable; semisun to semishade will give good results. Pot in a mix of equal parts soil, sand and peat moss; keep moist at all times—even wet. Propagate by dividing clumps in spring.

Airplane plant or **spider plant**, species of *Chlorophytum*, make splendid hanging baskets where the baby plants have space to "fly" away from the parent on the long slender stems. Tolerates sun, shade or in-between. Pot in a mix of equal parts soil, sand and peat moss; keep evenly moist. Cuttings root easily in water or moist potting soil at any season. Leaf tip dieback is usually caused by letting the soil get too dry between waterings. Keep airplane or spider plant out of reach of your cat or dog as they love to nibble on the leaves; the leaves are not toxic, however.

Aralia is the common name for *Dizygotheca elegantissima*. The name "aralia" is also applied to fatsia, polyscias, and tetrapanax. All are excellent foliage plants for indoors. The black-green leaves of dizygotheca are divided into nine segments with saw-toothed edges. *Polyscias filicifolia* has finely-cut foliage too, like a delicate fern. Fatsia and tetrapanax have bold, palmately lobed leaves. *Fatsia japonica* is outstanding greenery for an indoor planter. *Tetrapanax papyriferum* is the rice paper plant. Its young leaves are covered with white, feltlike material. Pot all in a mix of equal parts soil, sand and peat moss, and keep evenly moist. All will grow in semisun to semishade, but tetrapanax needs more sun. Polyscias likes 50 percent humidity, or more; the others will tolerate less. Provide average house warmth. Propagate by cuttings, preferably in spring.

Asparagus-fern is a tender relative of the hardy plant we cultivate outdoors in the vegetable garden. *A. plumosus* is the filmy green foliage much used by florists with roses. Its wiry, semiclimbing stems have prickles. *A. sprengeri* has coarser leaves than those of garden asparagus. It is a cast-iron house plant that can live through a little dryness (too much will cause the leaves or needles to turn yellow and fall from the plant), but not poorly drained soil. When really happy it will open fragrant white flowers in season, followed by red berries. For these and other house-plant asparagus, provide moist, loamy soil of equal parts sand, peat and garden soil; give average house warmth; sun to semishade. Propagate by division any time, or sow seeds in the spring.

Aspidistra is an old, old-fashioned plant hardly ever seen these days. But it should be, for it has a never-say-die disposition. Leaves are generally cornlike, often handsomely variegated with white or cream stripes. Aspidistra will grow in semi- to full shade, warmth of the average house and moist soil of equal parts loam, sand and peat moss. Start it in a good-sized pot, and don't bother to transplant more than once every second or third year. Propagate by division of roots in spring or summer.

Chinese evergreen is the popular name for aglaonema. It will grow for long periods of time in plain water. Some species are showier, having yellow or silver variegation on the leaves. All make outstanding plants indoors. Culture is easy to provide in the average house: warmth, shade, and moist soil of equal parts garden loam, sand and peat moss. Propagate by air-layering, tip cuttings or occasionally by division at any time except in late fall and early winter.

Coleus makes a Persian carpet of colors in the hybrid strains. Provide average house warmth, and several hours direct sun in winter. Pot in mix of equal parts soil, sand and peat moss and keep evenly moist. Keep pinching out the tips of new growth to promote bushiness. Watch out for mealybugs; they love coleus. Propagate any time by sowing seeds or taking cuttings; keep warm and moist.

Dracaenas are members of the lily family, and all, a varied lot, are grown for attractive foliage. When it comes to coping with air pollution, lack of bright light and general neglect, dracaenas are the real diehards among attractive foliage house plants. The corn-plant types—species and varieties of *D. fragrans*—are leafy and tall like a corn plant. The *godseffiana* types are entirely different, seldom more than 18 inches tall, usually with emerald leaves splashed and spotted with gold. *D. marginata* with its red-edged slender green leaves gives a stark, sometimes bizarre, appearance in older plants, because the branches zig-zag and contort strangely. Well grown and in the right kind of interior, *marginata* is handsome, but it does have a starkness that renders it more at home with contemporary, rather than with period, furnishings. Dracaenas will thrive in average house warmth, in semisun to shade. Pot in a mix of equal parts soil, sand and peat moss; keep moist. Feed every other week. Stem cuttings root easily in spring or summer.

Dumbcane, the common name for dieffenbachia, is appropriate because sap from the stems can cause temporary speechlessness when touched to the tongue (or worse—it is not something to fool around with). Dieffenbachias combine many shades of green, cream and white, with bold shape and growth habit. Kinds like Rudolph Roehrs, *D. amoena* and *D. picta* are the most beautiful. Provide warmth, semisun to semishade and pot in a mix of equal parts soil, sand and peat moss; keep moist. Propagate by air-layering at any time. Or, cut pieces of stem into 3-inch lengths in spring or summer, and root in water or in moist peat moss and sand in high humidity.

Ferns—in all shapes and forms we associate with the word "fern"—are available today in varieties that do well as house plants. The Boston fern is easy, and now there are other varieties of it to give added interest—especially finely cut and frilled types such as Fluffy Ruffles, Smithii and Whitmanii. The holly ferns (*Cyrtomium*) have leathery, hollylike leaves. Various kinds of polypodium and polystichum are excellent indoors. *Davallia* (rabbit's-foot), bird's-nest (*Asplenium*), staghorn (*Platycerium*) and *Pteris ensiformis victoriae* (Victorian table fern) also make beautiful house plants. Ferns need semisun to shade, combined with moist, humusy soil and average house temperatures. Moisture in the air around ferns helps them grow luxuriantly. Propagate by division in spring or early summer.

Ficus is the Latin name for common rubber tree, but it also represents several other species which are now probably more popular for indoor gardens. Weeping fig, for example, is perhaps the prettiest of all indoor trees. Fiddleleaf fig has large, durable, leathery leaves that grow to 18 inches long or more. And a new fig being introduced in plant shops, *F. triangularis*, has fascinating triangle-shaped leaves. Ficus, regardless of species, need average house warmth and sun to semishade. Pot in a mix of equal parts soil, sand and peat moss; keep evenly moist. Fertilize every other week in spring and summer; monthly or not at all in fall and winter. Propagate by air-layering or tip cuttings.

Fittonia or nerve plant makes a carpet of olive-green, papery-thin leaves netted with glowing rose-pink or creamy to silvery white veins. It needs warmth, high humidity and semisun to semishade. Especially suited to terrariums.

Gold-dust plant or aucuba is an evergreen shrub of value outdoors in mild climates, and highly ornamental for indoors. Its leathery leaves carry a high gloss, and have blotches of yellow. Pot in a mix of equal parts soil, sand and peat moss; keep evenly moist. Provide semisun to semishade and winter temperatures, ideally, between 55 and 65 degrees F. Propagate by cuttings at any time except winter.

Grape-ivy and related cissus are practically foolproof if given half a chance. They're prettiest when placed to cascade from a shelf, pedestal or hanging basket. Culture calls for average house warmth, a place in semisun to semishade. Pot in a mixture of equal parts soil, sand, peat moss and vermiculite; keep evenly moist. Propagate by cuttings in spring or summer.

Hawaiian ti, *Cordyline terminalis tricolor*, is a favorite and enduring foliage plant that forms a rosette of broad leaves. Basically these are green, but the variegation is free and unpredictable, usually cream, white, pink or rosy red. Grow the same as dracaena.

Ivy is a name applied to many different plants, but it properly belongs to members of the genus *Hedera*, best known in the species *helix*, English ivy. It is available in countless varieties. Some have typical English ivy leaves, except smaller—Merion Beauty, for example. Others have the same leaves, except they've been curled, waved and crinkled. Curlilocks is a lovely example. And some others have color variations, like the yellow-and-green California Gold. All are good climbers for indoors and will attach themselves by aerial roots to rough surfaces, such as a brick wall. And they are unsurpassed ground covers for large indoor planters. Perhaps best of all indoors, they are superb for hanging baskets, and to cascade from a bookshelf. Even in poor light a healthy plant of English ivy will be decorative for months on end—provided you never let the soil dry out. Grow English ivy in moist soil with average house warmth. English ivy thrives in almost all light situations from sunny to shady. Red spider-mites and scale may attack. To propagate, take 4-inch cuttings in spring or summer.

Jade plant, *Crassula argentea*, either thrives and becomes an old friend, or else it expires right away. It needs well-drained soil (equal parts soil, sand and peat), kept on the dry side, and at least a few hours direct sun each day. Mealybugs have a natural attraction and overwatering is another trap with jade plant. For best growth and coloring, grow in full sun indoors.

Norfolk Island pine, or *Araucaria excelsa*, is an evergreen tree for pots. It has tiers of densely needled branches. Give it a location where temperatures don't often exceed 75 degrees F. in winter, and where direct sun is available for two or three hours daily. Plant in equal parts soil, sand, peat moss and vermiculate and keep evenly moist.

Palms make slow-growing plants with the ability to withstand lack of light, drafts of cold, hot, or dry air—and neglect in general, but *not* soil allowed to dry out. The miniature palms (known variously by such names as *Neanthe bella, Collinia elegans* and correctly as *Chamaedorea elegans bella*) are useful for terrariums while they are seedlings. After a year or two they grow large enough for pot and planter use. The fish-tail palms (*Caryota*) are good for containers while young. The bamboo palm (*Chamaedorea erumpens*) is especially beautiful for rooms decorated in an Oriental manner. Other palms suited for indoors include the areca (don't ever let it dry out), kentia, rhapis and *Phoenix roebelenii* (dwarf date palm). Ideally, palms need sun to semishade with average house temperatures. Pot in a mix of equal parts soil, sand and peat moss and keep moist at all times. Feed every other week except in the dead of winter. Red spider-mites, mealybugs and scale may attack. Keep leaves sponged or showered clean.

Peperomia is one of the most popular small foliage plants. There are almost countless varieties on the market. Keep in average house warmth and in a location with semisun to semishade. Plant in a mix of equal parts soil, sand, peat moss and leaf mold and keep on the dry side, but not so dry that the leaves wilt. Overwatering results in root rot. Propagate by leaf or stem cuttings taken in spring or summer—or by division at any time the plant is making active growth.

Philodendrons, since the early 1940's, have come from near obscurity to become a household word. Ironically, two plants most generally known as philodendron are related, but known botanically by other names. One called ivy and pothos is *Scindapsus*; the other is *Monstera deliciosa*, variously called Swiss cheese plant and cutleaf philodendron.

Philodendron species divide themselves fairly neatly into two groups—those that climb and those that don't, called self-heading. The climbers need a moist totem pole to climb.

Materials for this support include pressed osmunda fiber and pieces of bark. Or you can make your own by wrapping a piece of 1/2-inch mesh chickenwire around unmilled sphagnum moss. The air roots of the philodendron will attach themselves to the totem.

Philodendrons thrive in average house warmth, and semisun to shade. They need humidity, but tolerate dry air if the growing medium (equal parts soil, sand, peat moss and vermiculite) is kept moist. Propagate at any time by air-layering or rooting cuttings of healthy growth.

Ponytail (*Beaucarnea recurvata*) grows to tree size indoors, forming a great water-reserving bulb that thrusts out of the soil. Give it some sun in average warmth. Pot in a mix of equal parts soil, sand and peat; keep on the dry side.

Prayer plant is the interesting common name for maranta. In the daytime its satiny foliage lies flat; at night the leaves turn upward. Grow it in all-purpose potting soil; keep evenly moist. Dry soil causes the leaf tips and edges to turn yellow, then brown and dead. High humidity and warmth promotes the best growth, in semishade to shade. Propagate by dividing old plants in spring or summer.

Purple passion and velvet plant are the common names for gynura, a hanging plant that needs sun to semisun and lots of pinching to promote compactness. Grow in a mix of equal parts soil, sand and peat moss; keep evenly moist. Give it average house warmth.

Schefflera, or umbrella-tree, makes a graceful, durable plant to 4 feet tall or more. The sizable scheffleras usually sold by florists almost always need a new pot an inch or two larger in diameter and some fresh soil. This is one of those indoor plants that grows like crazy for some persons, sulks and dies for others. It needs average house warmth, adapts to sun, also to semishade. Pot in a mix of equal parts soil, sand and peat moss. Here opinions vary—some say keep it on the dry side, others swear by watering heavily. What this probably means is that a plant which receives poor light should be kept on the dry side; a schefflera in a warm, sunny spot needs lots more water. Propagate by stem cuttings in spring.

Screw-pine, *Pandanus veitchii*, has rosettes of cornlike foliage with toothed edges, sometimes striped vertically with white. Grown to a single rosette, few plants rival the screw-pine in gracefulness when displayed indoors on a pedestal. Culture calls for average house warmth, and a place in semi-sun to semishade. Pot in a mix of equal parts soil, peat moss and sand; keep evenly moist. Propagate by removing side-shoots or suckers when they have leaves about 5 inches long. Root in moist vermiculite in high humidity.

Snake plant or sansevieria, is one of the toughest of all house plants. There are bird's-nest types only 6 inches tall, and others with sword-shaped leaves to 3 feet tall or more. Sometimes there are spikes of small white flowers that are sweetly fragrant. This plant is truly remarkable in that it will grow in full sun or full shade; in moist or dry soil; a cool room or a very warm place. Propagate by division or leaf cuttings in spring or summer. For best appearance, group several sansevierias together in matching or complimentary containers.

Spathiphyllum, like the philodendron, is one of those common plants that most of us know by its Latin name. Although we think of it generally as a foliage plant, spathiphyllum is in fact one of the best of all flowering plants to grow indoors. Varieties vary from 18 inches tall to 4 feet or more; the flowers, which are white spathes, from 2 inches to 12 inches long. Grow in a mixture of equal parts soil, sand, peat moss and vermiculite; keep evenly moist at all times. Provide semisun to shade, although greater light tends to encourage more flowers. It needs average house warmth; tolerates a dry atmosphere but thrives on 30 percent humidity or more.

Swedish-ivy or plectranthus is probably today's favorite hanging plant, along with wandering Jew, asparagus-fern and spider or airplane plant. It will grow in any bright window, from sunny to shady, in average house temperatures. Plant in a mixture of equal parts soil, sand, peat moss and vermiculite; keep evenly moist. Most important care for Swedish-ivy is to keep pinching out the growing tips—following the formation of every two to four pairs of new leaves. This encourages compact, bushy growth. Propagate by cuttings at any season; they root in a matter of days when placed in water, or you can insert them in a pot of moist potting soil and cover with a drinking glass or clear plastic bag for a few days until new roots take hold.

Tolmiea or piggyback plant makes a beautiful basket or you can display it on a pedestal so that the leaves can cascade gracefully. The common name comes from the plant's quaint habit of forming baby plants on top of the old leaves. Grow it in a mixture of equal parts soil, sand, peat moss and vermiculite; NEVER allow the soil to dry out severely. Needs semi-sun to shade. To propagate, pin an old leaf with a baby on top in a pot of moist soil placed alongside the parent plant. After it forms a root system, clip the stem that attaches it to the parent.

Wandering Jew is a common name applied to many members of the tradescantia family. All thrive in average house warmth, need bright light if not a few hours of direct sun, and humusy potting soil kept evenly moist. Like Swedish-ivy, frequent pinching out of the growing tips is the key to growing bushy, full wandering Jews. Cuttings root easily in water or moist vermiculite at any time.

Flowering House Plants

African violets, not true violets at all, are actually saintpaulias, plants that came originally from South Africa. Learn to grow them successfully and you can grow almost any flowering house plant. In winter African violets need at least 2 hours of direct sun in order to bloom well. In summer a bright north window will promote blooms. If you want to grow them in a sunny window, give the necessary shade by using a thin curtain, or setting them beneath taller, shade-giving, sun-loving plants. Provide evenly moist soil at all times and chances are they will thrive in average house humidity, but 35 percent or more is preferable when winter heat is on. Plant in soil from an African violet specialist, or mix your own, using equal parts potting soil, sand (or perlite), leaf mold (or peat moss) and vermiculite.

African violet pests include mealybugs, cyclamen mites and nematodes. Leaf spot and rings are caused by watering roots with icy water, or from getting cold water on the leaves themselves. Tepid water won't harm them. If plants grow weak and spindly and no flower buds form, make a quick check of your growing conditions. Chances are you need to provide more light, humidity, a temperature range between 70 and 75 degrees F. and evenly moist soil. If buds form, but fail to open, provide more humidity; be sure plants aren't in a cold, hot, or dry draft; don't get heavy handed with fertilizer —it won't correct poor growing conditions.

Propagate African violets at any time by taking leaf cuttings, dividing multiple-crowned plants, or rooting the sideshoots or suckers that form.

Amaryllis grow from bulbs available in flowering-size during fall and winter from local garden centers and by mail. Their growth cycle is fascinating. Every four healthy new leaves store up a scape of several flowers inside the bulb. With the neck portion of the bulb sticking out of the pot, plant in a mix of equal parts soil, sand and peat moss. Keep evenly moist at all times, and feed with liquid house-plant food every two weeks except in autumn. Then, let it be dry for at least two months, and do not apply fertilizer. The leaves will dry up and fall off. Shortly afterwards the flower bud will begin to show, at which time the pot should be moved to a growing spot with several hours sun or bright light all day and in average house warmth.

Aphelandra or zebra plant is pretty enough without flowers to compete with almost any flowering house plant. The glossy green leaves have distinctive and bright yellow veins. Give it a spot in morning or afternoon sun in winter, more shade in summer. Keep the soil evenly moist, but don't ever let aphelandra dry out severely. If you do, it will immediately drop a lot of leaves.

Begonias and variety are almost synonymous. First are the wax or semperflorens ("everblooming"). Seedlings or young plants from cuttings give the best performance. Showiest are today's F_1 hybrids, some with flowers to 2 inches across. Kinds with some leaves almost or entirely white are called calla-lily begonias. For neat growth and constant bloom, give lots of sunlight and feed every two weeks with house-plant fertilizer. Pot in a mix of equal parts soil, vermiculite, peat moss and sand. When plants grow tall and spindly, cut back old branches to the soil. This allows light and air to reach the new shoots that grow at the base. These will grow quickly into a vigorous, flower-covered plant.

The angel-wing begonias have handsome leaves, often silver-spotted, and in season clusters of pink, red, orange or white flowers. The stems are reminiscent of small bamboo canes. Similar are the hairy-leaved begonias with fuzzy leaves covered by tiny silvery or reddish hairs.

The beefsteak, star or rhizomatous begonias include miniatures the size of a tea-cup, as well as varieties with the commanding appearance of a large philodendron. Seasonal flowers are in delicate sprays of white or pale pink.

Rex begonias, technically also rhizomatous, are the most elegant of foliage fabrics—like fine silk or brocade, often with changeable colors according to the light striking the leaf surface. These need more moisture in the air around them, and when young and small can be cultivated in a terrarium. They need bright light, but not much direct sun. Rexes grow superbly in a fluorescent-light garden.

Bromeliads—showy, colorful, and even bizarre—share the common pineapple's habit of growing a rosette of tough, stiff or leathery leaves. As interesting, permanent accent plants for indoor gardening, the bromeliads are without equal. There are many kinds, but these are especially good ones which are easily obtainable in this country: *Aechmea*, the living vase plant, has outstanding foliage all year, plus showy flowers in season, followed by long-lasting scarlet berries. The common name refers to the leaf rosettes which have a long, slender tube from which the flower stem grows. In bloom, the plant appears to have provided its own vase, for the tube of leaves will hold water.

Billbergia, particularly the variety *nutans* (called queen's-tears), is widely grown and easy to obtain. Its rosettes are similar to a young pineapple, except they are longer and more slender. The pendant, graceful flowers have violet-edged green petals.

Cryptanthus stay within a few inches above the ground. In fact, their rosettes of leaves stay on such a horizontal plane that as a group they are called earth stars. Other bromeliads of special interest to indoor gardeners include those named dyckia, guzmania, neoregelia, nidularium, quesnelia and vriesia.

Bromeliad culture depends on a coarse, open growing medium, because most are air plants in their native haunts. Pot in a mix of equal parts peat moss and sand; or in unshredded sphagnum moss; or in osmunda fiber. Whichever medium you choose, keep it on the dry side; pay more attention to keeping the rosettes of leaves filled with water, but empty each time before you add a fresh supply. Bromeliads will grow in semisun to shade. Provide average house warmth. Blooming-size rosettes can be encouraged to bloom by this system: Enclose in a large plastic bag with a ripe Jonathan or Cortland apple for 48 hours. Chances are blooms will follow within 8 weeks following this treatment. Propagate bromeliads by rooting offsets from the base in a moist mix of peat moss and sand. (After flowering, many bromeliads die, so the nurture of the offsets is necessary to perpetuate the plant.)

Cacti are the least demanding of flowering house plants. Cactus gardening is not limited to strange shapes and sharp thorns. Some kinds have beautiful flowers, almost always characterized by extremely delicate petals and vivid colors. Especially choice for flowers are Paramount Hybrids, various kinds of rebutias, echinopsis, lobivias, and mammillarias. Give them sun and warmth, with sandy soil on the dry side— but don't neglect watering entirely. A little clay flowerpot on a window sill near the radiator gets drier in the winter than the Sahara. In cultivation, cacti will do better on geranium care, discussed later in this chapter.

Camellias are among the most beautiful of the evergreen shrubs grown outdoors in the South. In the North you can grow them as large pot or tub plants, if you have a cool, sunny place to keep them indoors in winter. There are hundreds of exquisite hybrids derived from *Camellia japonica* which can be cultivated indoors, as described in this chapter for gardenia.

Christmas cactus sets flower buds only when days are short, beginning in September and continuing past the middle of October. During this period, provide only natural daylight; any artificial light before sun-up, or after sundown, may delay or prevent flowering. Culture includes average house warmth, except cooler in the fall if possible, and a place in semisun to semishade. Pot in a mix of equal parts soil, sand, and peat moss: keep this evenly moist through the year, except on the dry side in autumn. Fertilize regularly except in the fall months. Propagate by stem cuttings inserted in a glass of water, or in damp sand, any time except autumn.

Citrus trees in dwarf varieties make great house plants. Besides shiny, dark green leaves, they have the delightful habit of flowering intermittently all year, creamy white blossoms with heady fragrance, followed by fruits. Select from dwarf limes, lemons, calamondins, tangerines and oranges. Grow them exactly as you would geraniums (also included in this chapter).

Clivia is an amaryllis relative with fans of dark green, leathery leaves. In spring or summer these provide a perfect foil for the strong, upright stems which are crowned by umbels of salmon-pink flowers. Pollinate them and reap further reward—the seeds are bright, cherry-red and stay on for many months. Provide average house warmth and a semi-sunny to semishady place. Pot in a mix of equal parts soil, sand, and peat moss: keep this on the dry side, except moist in spring and summer. Feed every other week during warm weather.

Columnea is a newly popular relative of the African violet, gloxinia, and episcia, all discussed in this chapter. It is one of the best of all hanging basket plants and will prove almost everblooming in a warm, moist atmosphere where it receives a few hours of sunlight.

Crown-of-thorns is a cactuslike relative of the poinsettia, known officially as *Euphorbia milii*. All it needs to thrive is average house warmth and at least an hour or two of strong sun. Grow and propagate as for geraniums.

Episcias are relatives of the African violet and gloxinia. They are grown first for beautiful foliage, but whenever days are sunny, the air warm and moist, they'll light a festival of scarlet, yellow, or blue flowers. Episcias are at best in hanging baskets, for, like strawberries, they have runners or stolons which cascade gracefully from the parent plant. Culture depends on warmth—episcias resent any temperature below 65 degrees. They need moist air, but will tolerate average house conditions if soil is kept evenly moist at all times. Pot in a mix of equal parts soil, sand, peat moss, and leaf mold (or vermiculite). Give a location in semisun to shade. They grow to perfection in fluorescent-light gardens. Propagate by pinning the stem of a stolon into a pot of moist soil. Soon roots will form and the new plant can be cut from the old.

Flamingo flower or anthurium has scarlet, pink, or white flowers resembling a calla-lily inside-out. Some varieties have handsomely veined heart-shaped leaves. It needs warmth, high humidity, and bright light—but not much direct sun. Keep soil evenly moist. Propagate by division.

Flowering maple is an old favorite flowering house plant that can be trained to treelike height and shape. The common name comes from the maple-shaped leaves. Actually, flowering maple is a hibiscus relative, officially an abutilon. Hybrids like Apricot have big, pendant, bell-shaped flowers. Some kinds might be grown for their beautifully variegated leaves even if they never produce a bloom. Grow and propagate exactly as a geranium.

Fuchsias have elegant hanging blooms, often bi-colored. They need a cool, moist climate, and unless you can provide a window sill or indoor gardening spot with coolness at night in winter (65 degrees F. or less), you'd best grow fuchsias outdoors in a cool, shady place in summer, and buy new plants each spring. Pot in a mix of equal parts soil, sand and peat moss; keep this evenly moist. Feed whenever growing conditions are good, and plants are in active growth. Cut or pinch fuchsias back to induce new growth and flower buds. Stem cuttings may be rooted in late winter or spring.

Gardenias have a reputation for being just about the most temperamental of all flowering house plants. However, if you can get one—especially *Gardenia radicans floreplena* or *G. jasminoides veitchii*—to hang in long enough, it will likely adapt and even thrive for you. Culture depends first on a temperature range of 62 to 72 degrees F. in winter; cooler or warmer temperatures may damage the plant. Pot in a mix of equal parts soil, sand and German or Canadian peat moss; keep this evenly moist.

From January to September feed every other week with a solution made by mixing one ounce ammonium sulfate in two gallons of water. Locate plant in a sunny to semisunny place in winter; semishade to full shade in summer. Hot, dry air will cause gardenia leaf tips to turn black. Cold may cause leaves to turn yellow. Gardenia plants benefit from being showered weekly with tepid water under the kitchen faucet, or in the bathtub. Propagate by taking 6-inch stem cuttings in spring or summer. Insert in a mix of peat moss and sand; cover with a plastic bag until roots form.

Geraniums appeal to almost everyone. If you like to collect things, then geraniums are for you. There are thousands of species and named varieties, each slightly different. You could go one step further and collect only dwarfs, or only scented-leaf kinds. Common geranium hybrids of *Pelargonium hortorum* are often called zonal because of the darker green or reddish-brown zone in each leaf. Dwarf geraniums stay under 8 inches tall and will grow for months, even years, in a 3-inch pot. They require the same treatment as large geraniums, but are also suited to a fluorescent-light garden. Fancy-leaf geraniums belong in the same class with common kinds. They have bi- or tri-colored leaves, often in rich bronzes, scarlets and creamy whites or pale greens.

Ivy-leaf geraniums, varieties of *Pelargonium peltatum*, bear leathery leaves with a shape uncannily like that of English ivy, to which they are in no way related. They are great for hanging baskets. The flowers, often veined with a darker shade of their color, come in showy clusters, sometimes nearly smothering the plant in blooms.

Scented-leaf geraniums, beginning with the common "rose," *Pelargonium graveolens*, would be favorites even if they didn't bloom, because the foliage is a pleasant experience in fragrance whenever it is brushed. Collect kinds distinctly scented lemon, peppermint, apple, nutmeg, orange, strawberry, pineapple or ginger.

There are all kinds of odd-ball geraniums: there's the group with prickly stems, called cactus. A variety called Poinsettia has red or pink petals that are quilled and squarish, of different lengths. Jeanne has single, salmon-pink flowers pinked along the edges like a sweet William. Then there are bird's-egg with speckled petals, phlox-eyed flowers and rosebud geraniums, climbers, and still others.

Geranium culture starts with sun—several hours in fall

and winter in order to grow neatly and bloom. Average house warmth suits them, although long periods over 75 degrees F. won't help in winter. Pot in a mix of three parts soil to one of vermiculite or peat moss, plus one of sand. If your soil is clayish, use equal parts soil, sand and peat moss. To each 5-inch pot of this mix, add one teaspoon steamed bone meal. Keep geranium soil on the dry side; that is, water well, then not again until the surface soil is approaching dryness. Propagate by cuttings inserted in moist sand at any time. Cut them with a sharp knife, then lay in shady, airy place for an hour or two so that a callus can form over cut end; then insert in sand.

Gloxinias are velvety-leaved members of the gesneriad family, the same royal clan to which African violets belong. They are known botanically as *Sinningia*, although there is a true *Gloxinia* in the same family, just to confuse things. In practice, growers tend to call the natural species sinningias, the big-flowered hybrids gloxinias. Hybrid gloxinias flower in countless colors and combinations, including petals banded with contrasting color or white, and solid-color petals heavily spotted or misted with another color. They may be saucer- or cup-shaped, single or double.

Gloxinias need more sun than African violets—full to semisun in winter; semishade in summer. They need at least 40 percent humidity to bloom well; more is better. Pot the tubers in fall, winter or spring, covering the tops with about a half inch of soil. Use a mix of equal parts soil, sand, peat moss and vermiculite; keep this evenly moist at all times. After blooming stops, and leaf growth seems to have reached a standstill, gradually withhold water until stems and leaves die down; put pot and contents in cool, dark, mouseproof place for two to four months while the tuber rests.

During this time, keep soil barely moist so that the tuber won't shrivel. After the resting period, repot in fresh soil, move to light and warmth; provide moisture. Feed gloxinias in active growth. Thrips and mealybugs may attack. Gloxinia flower buds may turn brown and fail to open from too much water; not enough water; not enough moisture in the air; not enough light; too much fertilizer; or damage from the tiny, black, threadlike thrips insect.

Propagate by leaf cuttings taken from plant in active

growth. Insert stem 1 inch deep in moist peat moss and sand. A new tuber will form, which, after several weeks, can be potted separately. Sow seeds in late winter, spring or early summer for blooms about eight months later.

Ginger, especially the red *Alpinia purpurata*, is a large, leafy, tropical-looking plant that thrives in a warm, moist place. Give it some direct sunlight, a large tub and a growing mix of equal parts soil, sand, peat moss and vermiculite. Feed and water freely during the summer months.

Goldfish plant is known officially as hypocyrta. It makes a fascinating small hanging basket, and thrives with the same care as its more famous relative, the African violet.

Haemanthus, sometimes called blood-lily, is a handsome relative of the amaryllis. It grows from a bulb, and is cultivated the same as amaryllis.

Hibiscus—these flamboyant flowers make a super show in a window garden that is sunny and warm in winter. Flowers to dinner-plate size may be red, pink, orange, yellow, salmon or white. They grow on woody shrubs, and flower buds come on the new wood so that the plants can be pruned to compact, small proportions for indoor use, and blooms are still possible every day of the year. Keep soil evenly moist; otherwise, grow and propagate hibiscus the same as geraniums.

Impatiens, or sultanas, are the superstars for coloring shady summer gardens outdoors. Indoors they may not be so easy, because hot, dry air combined with impatiens makes a perfect home for red spider-mites. To grow impatiens indoors, provide moderate temperatures (62 to 72 degrees F. in winter) and a partly sunny place. Pot in a mix of equal parts soil, sand, peat moss and vermiculite; keep this evenly moist. Dip foliage in water of room temperature and swish it around at least once a week to discourage red spider-mites. Propagate by sowing seeds in late winter or early spring, or by inserting cuttings in a glass of water or in moist sand and peat moss in any season.

Kalanchoe include handsome foliages and fascinating flowering plants, especially varieties of the *blossfeldiana* type and species like *K. flammea* and *K. uniflora*. The hanging bell-shaped flowers, or upward facing clusters of starry blooms, may be vivid scarlet, or in subtle shades of yellow, bronze, apricot or mauve. Flowers in some make their appearance after the buds have been initiated by the shortest days of the year. Kalanchoes grow to perfection when given geranium culture.

Lantana, of the verbena family, is perhaps better for sun-baked places outdoors in summer than for a window garden. To winter lantanas indoors, start with rooted cuttings in autumn, or large plants cut back to shapeliness. Pot in a mix of equal parts soil, sand and peat moss. Keep this nicely moist through the winter, and, if possible, situate the plants in coolness—60 to 70 degrees F.—and in full sun. Thus grown, blooms will begin to appear by mid-winter and continue at increasing profuseness until planting time outdoors in the spring. Flowers may be yellow, pink, orange, dark rose or white, even lavender-blue in the hanging basket form. White flies are the bane of lantanas. Propagate by stem cuttings inserted in moist sand and peat moss in late summer or spring.

Lipstick plant or aeschynanthus is one of the best of all flowering hanging baskets. Give it a few hours of sun in a warm window, in African-violet soil, kept moist, and it will bloom off and on all the time. In some varieties the fuzzy red buds grow out of waxy brown calyxes, giving rise to the name "lipstick plant."

Orchids may be better house plants than you ever imagined. Best kinds for beginners include cattleya, epidendrum, oncidium, phalaenopsis and paphiopedilum. Study catalogs from orchid growers and you'll find other species and varieties recommended as house plants—*Brassavola nodosa*, for example, is a great orchid for growing as an indoor plant.

Orchid culture varies from one kind to another. In general they require a moist atmosphere and a sunny to semisunny place in winter, with somewhat less direct sun in the summer. Some kinds are grown in osmunda fiber, shredded redwood bark, or other coarse, fast-draining materials. Others are grown in sphagnum moss, or in a regular mix of equal parts soil, sand, peat moss and vermiculite. Temperature requirements are different too, but usually a range of 62 to 75 degrees F. is acceptable. If you can provide these conditions, then your investment in orchid literature and plants should be highly rewarding.

Oxalis have cloverlike leaves which fold up at night, open again each morning. Even those grown in fluorescent-light gardens close up at sundown. Many make outstanding potted plants indoors; they are elegant basket plants, too. Colors include white, pink, nearly red and yellow. Provide average house warmth and a sunny location. Pot in a mix of equal parts soil, sand, peat moss and vermiculite; keep this moist, except on the dry side while plants rest in summer. Oxalis are best acquired in summer or early fall; most kinds begin a period of strong growth in autumn. Propagate by dividing the tuberous roots or bulbs in summer.

Shrimp plant has curious bracts which may remind you of real shrimp. From these, small white flowers, typical of the mint family, are borne. After the flowers are gone the bracts hold on for many weeks. It is not unusual for shrimp plant (*Beloperone guttata*) to be in bloom constantly year after year. The original species has pinkish bronze bracts; Yellow Queen is chartreuse. Good for pots and baskets in a sunny place all winter; great outdoors in summer. Pinch out growing tips from time to time to encourage neat growth. Grow shrimp plant exactly the same as a geranium.

Wax plant is the appropriate common name for species of hoya—all plants with showy clusters of fragrant flowers that are truly waxlike. Thick, leathery leaves on twining stems may be plain green, but more likely streaked and splashed in silver, or boldly variegated creamy white, pale green, and glowing rose-pink. After blooms drop, do not remove the stem from which they came; this is called a spur, and future flower buds will develop from it. Stem cuttings inserted in moist sand or water root easily. Culture for the wax plant is the same as that for geraniums.

How to Care for Flowering Gift Plants

When you receive a potted gift plant which came from a humid, cool greenhouse, do your best to duplicate these conditions in your home. The first thing you can do is provide the plant with plenty of water. By the time a greenhouse "finishes" a plant—that is, brings it to full bloom and foliage—the soil of the pot is usually filled with roots; it will be using lots of water to keep the leaves and flowers full of life-giving moisture. Keep gift plants out of cold, dry and hot drafts of air. In winter give them a few hours of sun if possible, preferably in the morning. During warm seasons, keep gift plants in bright light, but avoid locations where direct sun would burn them. When a gift plant has many unopened buds, you can help them open by providing good cultural conditions, and by feeding every other week with a water-soluble house-plant fertilizer such as 15-5-5.

Azaleas of the more tender types known as Indica and Kurume are forced by florists. Temperatures below 20 degrees will harm them. When you receive one, keep the soil moist at all times. Shower the leaves with water at the kitchen sink, or in the bathtub, as often as possible. Coolness (55-65 degrees F.) will prolong the flowering season. Provide bright light all day, or direct sun early in the morning, or in late afternoon. Feed every week with half-strength house-plant fertilizer.

After the flowers fade, repot into a container 1 to 3 inches larger. Use a moist mix of soil, sand and Canadian or German peat moss. If there are wisps of branches sticking out here and there from the plant, snip them off. When the weather is warm outdoors, you can set the azalea in place outdoors protected from drying winds, and in semi- to full shade. If foliage shows any yellow in the summer, apply an iron chelate according to directions on the package. Bring the plant inside before frost. It will need evenly moist soil, a moist, cool atmosphere, and some sun. If you provide these conditions, your azaleas will be covered with bloom by the New Year, and will continue for several weeks.

Chrysanthemums will last days, even weeks longer, if you keep the soil constantly moist, and give them a little sun. Coolness helps the flowers stay fresh. After the blooms dry up, it is best to discard the plant; florist mums do not usually make good garden plants. Think of them rather as unusually long-lasting bouquets.

Cyclamen needs constantly moist soil. Keep it out of cold, dry, or hot drafts of air, in a spot that receives some sunlight. New flower buds will be promoted if you apply liquid fertilizer every two or three weeks. A temperature range of 62 to 72 degrees F. is appropriate.

Poinsettias like a warm place out of all drafts. Keep the soil constantly moist. They'll drop leaves if the soil dries severely, or if temperatures drop below 50 degrees F. When the colorful flowerlike bracts drop, set the plant away in a basement or in a cool, frost-free room, and let the soil be nearly dry until spring. Then bring to sunny warmth, water well and watch for new growth.

At this point with poinsettias you can go two ways. The easiest is to chop back all canes to 6 inches from the pot rim. From these, new stems will grow. At the same time, you can repot to new soil (equal parts soil, sand and peat moss). The other way with poinsettias gives you the satisfaction of rooting cuttings and multiplying the original plant to several. Here's how: Cut back the branches in spring to 6 inches, and when new growth is 6 to 10 inches tall, make cuttings of this new wood, allowing each to be at least 5 inches long. Clip off lower leaves and insert the stem 2 inches deep in moist peat moss and sand. Cover the cuttings with a large plastic bag and keep moist until they've made new roots; then pot up, either separately in a 5-inch pot, or three in a triangle in an 8-inch pot. You can grow poinsettias indoors all summer, in a sunny location, or they can be planted outdoors in a protected place with early morning or late afternoon sun. Whether you use the first or second method, after new growth is 6 to 10 inches tall, pinch out the tips to cause branching. Bring poinsettias indoors in autumn when nights begin to cool—usually September even in the South. Poinsettias bloom when days are short, so from mid-September to November, take care that they receive *no* artificial light from sundown to sun-up. This will assure flowering plants for Christmas.